THE
JESUS
WAY

CASEY S. PUTNEY

Edited by Kristen Defevers

Cover Design and Interior Formatting by KUHN Design Group | kuhndesigngroup.com

The Jesus Way: Returning to God's Design for Leadership
Copyright © 2025 by Casey Putney
Published by The Engagement Institute, LLC
Bellevue, Nebraska

ISBN (Hardback): 979-8-9992257-0-2
ISBN (Paperback): 979-8-9992257-1-9
ISBN (eBook): 979-8-9992257-2-6

Subjects: Leadership; Christianity; Spiritual Growth; Mindset; Personal Development

First Edition: 2025

Printed in the United States of America

*To Shannon, my queen, my anchor, and my encourager
through the quiet season God used to prepare me.*

To Mom, for a lifetime of love and support.

To Jasmine and Jadon, for being the reasons I pursued God.

CONTENTS

INTRODUCTION

Have you felt it?

That quiet, persistent whisper deep in your soul.

It's not loud.

It doesn't demand your attention.

But it's steady.

Unshakable.

A nudge that refuses to let you settle for less than the impact you were created to make.

It stirs in quiet moments.

It ignites a longing.

> To lead.

> To serve.

> To leave a mark that outlasts your own story.

That whisper isn't random. **It's God.**

And He's calling you to something bigger than yourself.

Drawing you toward a purpose greater than you can imagine.

And His calling is why you're holding this book in your hands right now.

Because leadership isn't about fame.

It's not about titles, applause, or recognition.

It's about something far deeper.

It's about stepping into the lives of others and making them better.

Stronger.

More hopeful.

It's about leading in a way that doesn't just change workplaces but instead—

Transforms hearts, families, and communities.

You've been placed where you are for a reason.

And that reason starts with the impact God means for you to have on the lives around you.

But will you lean in?

Will you listen?

Will you let God guide you toward that calling?

Listening to that whisper isn't easy.

The noise of life is loud.

Distractions pile up.

Doubts creep in.

Fear will tell you that you're not ready. You're not equipped. The path ahead is too uncertain.

But here's the truth:

God doesn't call the qualified.

He qualifies the called.

That whisper in your soul?

It's not asking you to have all the answers.

It's not waiting for you to be perfect.

It's simply asking you to trust and take one step forward.

This journey isn't about perfection.

It's about surrender.

It's not about proving your worth.

It's about embracing your purpose.

You may stumble.

You may question.

But don't let that stop you.

Faith isn't about having a clear road map.

It's about trusting the One who holds the map.

Obedience often feels like walking in the dark.

But God never asks you to move the mountain alone.

He simply asks you to take the first step toward it.

God has been preparing you for this moment.

Through every success.

Through every setback.

Through every joy and heartbreak.

Nothing in your life has been wasted.

The path forward may feel uncertain.

But when you walk in obedience to the calling God has placed on your life,

He will provide the strength, the wisdom, and the grace you need to fulfill it.

This book is an invitation.

A call to examine your heart.

To renew your mind.

To align your actions with the purpose God has for you.

Through each chapter, you'll uncover truths that will challenge you.

Inspire you.

Transform you.

Because leadership is not just a role.

It's a responsibility.

A responsibility to lead with:

> Humility
>
> Grace
>
> Unwavering faith

If you've ever doubted your ability to lead, you are not alone.

But doubt is not the end of your story.

It's the beginning of your reliance on God.

He sees the leader within you.

Even when you don't.

Even when you question yourself.

Even when you feel unqualified.

As you read this book, my prayer is that you will begin to see yourself as God sees you.

Chosen.

Equipped.

Ready to rise.

Ready to lead.

Ready to leave an impact that echoes beyond your lifetime.

The whisper that brought you here?

It's calling you to something extraordinary.

The question is: Will you answer?

THE FOUNDATION OF THE JESUS WAY

Jesus didn't start His ministry with commands.

He didn't start with rules.

He didn't start by telling people what to do.

He started by changing how they think.

The first words of His greatest sermon—the Sermon on the Mount—weren't about behavior.

They were about mindset.

Because Jesus knew—

Before you can lead differently, you must think differently.

The Beatitudes aren't just beautiful poetry.

They aren't just spiritual ideals.

They are a road map for leadership transformation.

This is where the Jesus Way begins.

Not with power, control, or authority.

Not with tactics, strategies, or leadership hacks.

But with a radical redefinition of success.

Jesus flipped the entire leadership model upside down.

He didn't say,

"Blessed are the strong."

"Blessed are the dominant."

"Blessed are those who demand respect."

He said,

"Blessed are the poor in spirit."

"Blessed are those who mourn."

"Blessed are the meek."

"Blessed are those who hunger and thirst for righteousness."

This wasn't just a sermon. It was a revolution.

WHY MINDSET COMES FIRST

The world teaches leadership from the outside in.

It tells you to fix your behavior, master the strategy, and play the game.

But Jesus teaches leadership from the inside out.

Because a renewed mind doesn't just change how you act.

It changes who you are.

And when your mind is renewed, your leadership becomes impossible to ignore.

People will see the difference.

They will see peace where there should be stress.

They will see confidence where there should be fear.

They will see humility where there should be pride.

This is why Jesus started here.

Because without a transformed mind, nothing else will last.

THE LEADERSHIP REVOLUTION BEGINS HERE

We aren't just reading these words.

We're rebuilding how we lead.

Each Beatitude is a mindset shift—

A new way to think, a new way to live, and a new way to lead.

A renewed mind is how we begin.

It's the first step in the Jesus Way.

The first step toward leadership that transforms.

The question is: Are you ready to think differently?

Because once you do—

You will never lead the same again.

THE INNER REVOLUTION

CHAPTER ONE

LESS OF ME, MORE OF GOD

"Blessed are the poor in spirit,
for theirs is the kingdom of heaven."
MATTHEW 5:3

WHAT DOES "POOR IN SPIRIT" MEAN?

When Jesus declared, "Blessed are the poor in spirit,"

He wasn't glorifying weakness.

He was launching a revolution in leadership.

To be poor in spirit is to recognize our absolute dependence on God.

It's the moment you realize:

Your talent is not enough.

Your strategy is not enough.

Your effort is not enough.

Because nothing can substitute for the wisdom, strength, and peace that God provides.

This is where leadership truly begins:

Not in the pursuit of personal greatness

But in the surrender of your ego.

This is what sets kingdom leaders apart.

The moment you embrace this mindset, you stop leading alone.

You step into a divine partnership.

And that changes everything.

LEADERSHIP STARTS WITH EMPTYING YOURSELF

The world teaches leaders to build themselves up.

Fight for recognition.

Control the outcomes.

Prove your worth.

But Jesus offers a radical alternative.

True success comes not from inflating yourself but from emptying yourself.

A leader who is poor in spirit makes space for God's wisdom to flow through them.

They don't fight to be the smartest person in the room.

They don't lead from insecurity or ego.

They don't measure their value by titles, applause, or achievement.

Instead, they trust. They listen. They surrender.

And in doing so, they discover a confidence that ego can never provide.

THE WORLD TEACHES SELF-RELIANCE, BUT JESUS TEACHES SURRENDER

Everything in our culture tells us to depend on ourselves.

"Be self-sufficient."

"Be independent."

"Believe in yourself."

But Jesus flips this upside down.

He says the greatest blessing comes not from self-sufficiency

But from surrender.

To be poor in spirit is to acknowledge:

"I don't have all the answers, but God does."

"I don't have to carry everything because God carries me."

"My success is not about my strength—it's about my obedience."

The poor in spirit aren't without strength.

They are strong because they know their strength comes from God Himself.

And Jesus promises that those who embrace this mindset…

Will inherit the kingdom of heaven.

WHAT DOES "FOR THEIRS IS THE KINGDOM OF HEAVEN" MEAN?

Jesus isn't just talking about life after death.

The kingdom of heaven is not only a future reward.

It's a reality we step into now.

The moment you stop relying on yourself and start trusting in God—

You begin to experience His power, His provision, and His peace.

Being poor in spirit doesn't mean losing control and becoming powerless.

It means releasing control and making space for God's power to lead.

Because when you stop carrying leadership alone

God steps in to lead with you.

And when God leads, your influence grows beyond anything you could build on your own.

And when your influence grows, it doesn't just elevate you.

It lifts those around you.

It brings healing, clarity, and hope.

TWO GIFTS FOR LEADERS WHO ARE POOR IN SPIRIT

Clarity.

When you are poor in spirit, the noise fades.

You stop performing.

You stop posturing.

You stop grasping for identity in the eyes of others.

And suddenly—everything becomes clear.

You see God more vividly.

You hear Him more clearly.

You follow Him more freely.

Because your hands are no longer full of yourself.

Confidence.

The world says confidence comes from credentials, charisma, and control.

But true confidence comes from surrender.

Because once you've let go of your need to prove yourself—

You become unshakable.

You no longer lead from fear of failure.

You lead from trust.

From peace.

From the steady knowledge that your strength is not your own.

And that is the kind of leader the world cannot ignore.

Leaders who grasp this do not second-guess themselves.

They do not lead from insecurity.

They move forward with boldness.

Not because they know everything

But because they trust the One who does.

THE KINGDOM IS YOURS, RIGHT NOW

Jesus is not promising a distant blessing.

He is inviting you into a new way of living and leading.

One that is not built on pressure, fear, or the need to prove yourself.

When you are poor in spirit, you step into a life where peace replaces anxiety and confidence replaces insecurity.

The kingdom of heaven belongs to those who stop striving for control and start trusting in the power of God.

This is not just good news. It is life-changing.

But Jesus didn't just teach this mindset, He lived it as well. Let's step into His experience.

JESUS IN THE WILDERNESS

The desert is silent, but the silence is not peaceful.

It is heavy, pressing down like the weight of the sun above.

The air is thick with heat, the kind that steals breath and drains strength.

The wind, though faint, carries the scent of dry earth and loneliness.

For forty days, Jesus has been here. Alone.

His body is weak. His stomach, empty.

Hunger gnaws at Him, a dull ache at first, now an all-consuming pain.

His skin is rough from the sun's relentless fire.

His human body craves food, rest, and relief.

Yet here He remains, waiting.

Preparing.

A shadow moves among the rocks. A presence lingers, unseen but felt.

The stillness is broken by a voice.

"If you are the Son of God, tell these stones to become bread."

The words slither into the air, soft but sharp.

The offer is simple.

Just one word, one act, and the pain will end.

The hunger will be gone.

The weakness, removed.

The voice does not shout. It whispers, feeding the ache, playing on the frailty of the moment.

Jesus' lips are cracked and dry, but He speaks with steady strength.

"It is written: 'Man shall not live on bread alone, but on every word that comes from the mouth of God.'"

His stomach screams for relief, but His soul is full.

He will not act apart from the Father.

The presence shifts.

The ground beneath Him seems to dissolve, and suddenly,

He stands at the highest point of the temple in Jerusalem.

Below, the city stirs.

People move through the streets, unaware of the battle unfolding above them.

The voice returns, this time laced with persuasion.

"If you are the Son of God, throw yourself down. For it is written: 'He will command his angels concerning you, and they will lift you up in their hands.'"

It is a challenge, a test wrapped in scripture.

A chance to prove Himself, to make heaven respond.

One leap, and the angels will come. The people below will witness His power.

Recognition.

Validation.

Proof.

Jesus does not waver. His voice does not tremble.

"It is also written: 'Do not put the Lord your God to the test.'"

The presence grows restless.

The air thickens again. The desert shifts, and now they stand upon a high mountain.

The world stretches below them.

Kingdoms.

Riches.

Power.

Everything the eyes can see.

"All this I will give you if you will bow down and worship me."

For a moment, the offer hangs between them.

The hunger remains. The exhaustion lingers.

The path before Jesus is clear.

He has come to establish a kingdom.

The cross looms ahead. The suffering, the rejection, and the pain can all be avoided.

One moment of surrender.

One act of submission.

The kingdoms of the world would be His without the agony of what is to come.

Jesus lifts His head. His eyes burn, not with hunger, but with fire. His voice cuts through the air.

"Away from me, Satan! For it is written: 'Worship the Lord your God, and serve him only.'"

The presence recoils. The weight lifts. The silence returns.

And then, the wind shifts.

A gentle breeze brushes against Jesus' face.

The test is over.

The battle, won.

Angels appear. Their hands, light upon His shoulders. Their voices, soft with comfort.

Strength returns.

Jesus has not lost.

He has not bent.

He has not relied on Himself.

He has remained poor in spirit, fully dependent on the Father.

And because of that, He walks forward, not in defeat, but in power.

THE ULTIMATE EXAMPLE OF BEING POOR IN SPIRIT

Jesus had every reason to rely on Himself.

But He didn't.

He could have turned the stones into bread.

He could have tested God for validation.

He could have taken the kingdoms of the world without the cross.

But in every test, He remained poor in spirit.

He didn't act apart from the Father.

He didn't take shortcuts.

He didn't force control.

He trusted.

THIS IS THE FIRST STEP IN THE JESUS WAY

This is not just a better way to lead.

This is a better way to live.

The world says lead with power.

Jesus says lead with trust.

The world says take control.

Jesus says let go and follow Me.

The world says prove yourself.

Jesus says rest in who I made you to be.

This Beatitude is the foundation of the Jesus Way.

Because until we empty ourselves, we cannot be filled.

Until we let go of self-reliance, we cannot experience God's provision.

The Jesus Way always begins with the heart of the leader, but it never ends there.

When a leader becomes poor in spirit, those they lead begin to experience something rare.

A culture of pressure gives way to a culture of peace.

Ego is replaced with humility.

The atmosphere shifts.

The weight lifts.

And little by little, the lives around them begin to change.

Not because the leader tried to change others,

But because they first allowed God to change them.

This is where the revolution begins.

Less of me. More of God.

CHAPTER TWO

WHEN THE STORM COMES

"Blessed are those who mourn,
for they will be comforted."

MATTHEW 5:4

WHAT DOES "MOURNING" REALLY MEAN?

Leadership is not a journey of uninterrupted success.

It is a path filled with triumphs and trials, victories and disappointments.

Many see setbacks as interruptions to leadership.

But the renewed embrace a different perspective:

Struggles are not disruptions to the journey.

They are the journey.

The way a leader navigates difficulty determines their impact and reveals their strength.

This is the foundation of Jesus' words:

"Blessed are those who mourn, for they will be comforted."

Mourning is not just about grief.

It is about what we do when life and leadership threaten to overwhelm us.

The world teaches leaders to hide their pain. Jesus teaches us to bring it to God.

Most people associate mourning with loss.

But its meaning runs deeper.

Mourning is the honest acknowledgment that we are not in control.

It is realizing that our strength alone is not enough.

The world teaches leaders to:

Suppress emotions.

Push through struggles.

Appear strong—no matter what.

But Jesus teaches the opposite.

Mourning is not weakness.

It is an invitation to bring our

Sorrow

Frustration

Disappointments

To God—rather than carrying them alone.

The blessing is not in the pain itself.

The blessing is in the partnership with God that pain invites us into.

THE RHYTHM OF LEADERSHIP

Leadership is like the rhythm of the tides.

High-tide moments are seasons of abundance.

Success overflows.

Momentum builds.

It feels like nothing can go wrong.

But just as surely—low tide comes.

Progress stalls.

Challenges mount.

What once worked no longer seems to.

Wise leaders do not expect constant abundance.

Instead, they prepare their hearts and minds for both seasons.

High tide teaches gratitude.

Low tide teaches trust.

Mourning in the low tide is not despair. It is bringing our empty nets to God and trusting that He will fill them again.

EMPTY NETS AND UNSHAKEN FAITH

Imagine a fisherman returning from the sea with empty nets.

He does not throw them aside in frustration.

He does not abandon his work.

Instead, he prepares them for the next day,

Trusting that the ocean will provide again.

As leaders, our empty nets represent:

When our best efforts seem to yield nothing.

When plans falter.

When progress disappears.

These moments can be discouraging.

But they are also opportunities.

Leadership is not about having all the answers.

It is about having the faith to lay our struggles at God's feet.

When we trust Him with our emptiness—

He doesn't just refill our nets,

He transforms our perspective.

He gives us the strength to try again.

He gives us the wisdom to lead with renewed purpose.

GREAT LEADERS DON'T IGNORE THE STORM, THEY SHOW OTHERS HOW TO NAVIGATE IT

Leaders don't inspire by pretending struggles don't exist.

They inspire by showing how to walk through them with faith.

Mourning with God is not about dwelling in sorrow.

It is about moving through difficulty with trust.

Some leaders let struggle defeat them.

Others let struggle refine them.

Jesus promises that those who mourn will be comforted.

Not because their hardships will disappear instantly.

But because they will no longer carry them alone.

Leadership is not about avoiding challenges.

It is about knowing where to take them when they come.

JESUS WEEPING AT LAZARUS' TOMB

The road to Bethany was quiet.

The disciples followed behind Jesus, uneasy.

They knew why they were here.

The message had come days ago: Lazarus was sick.

But Jesus had not rushed to his side.

And now, it was too late.

Martha greeted Him first.

Her voice trembled with faith and heartbreak.

"Lord, if you had been here, my brother would not have died."

Jesus met her eyes, filled with understanding.

"Your brother will rise again."

Martha nodded, her theology intact.

"I know he will rise again in the resurrection at the last day."

But Jesus spoke something deeper.

"I am the resurrection and the life. The one who believes in me will live, even though they die."

Then Mary arrived.

She said the same words her sister had spoken—

"Lord, if you had been here, my brother would not have died."

But what followed was different.

She did not speak of theology.

She did not speak of the future.

She wept.

Her grief was raw, broken, and full of pain.

And then—silence.

The kind of silence that holds pain too deep for words.

Jesus looked around.

He saw the tears streaming down Mary's face.

He saw the crowd of mourners wailing in sorrow.

He saw the sealed tomb—cold and final.

And then, Jesus wept.

The Son of God wept.

Not out of hopelessness.

Not out of defeat.

But because He stepped fully into the moment.

He did not rush past sorrow.

He did not dismiss the pain.

He felt it.

And then—He took it to the Father.

"Father, I thank you that you have heard me."

"I knew that you always hear me."

With those words, He turned mourning into faith.

He placed the weight in the hands of God.

Then, with a voice that thundered through death itself—

"Lazarus, come out!"

And the man who had been dead walked out of the tomb.

THREE LEADERSHIP LESSONS FROM JESUS' MOURNING

Jesus didn't avoid pain.

He stepped into it.

He didn't rush to fix it.

He stayed present with it.

And that teaches us something profound.

1. A leader doesn't have to have the answers—

They have to show up.

2. A leader doesn't have to remove every burden—

They have to carry it alongside others.

3. A leader doesn't have to silence sorrow—

They have to create space for it to breathe.

Jesus didn't just weep.

He revealed the heart of God through His tears.

And that kind of mourning?

It doesn't weaken leadership—

It deepens it.

WHAT DOES "THEY WILL BE COMFORTED" MEAN?

Comfort is not escape.

It is not pretending the pain isn't real.

It is not a spiritual shortcut or a positive spin.

When Jesus says, "They will be comforted,"

He is not offering surface-level relief.

He is offering His presence.

His power.

His peace.

This comfort does not come through avoiding mourning—

It comes amid the pain.

It meets us in the broken places.

In the silence.

In the moments we stop leading and just begin to weep.

And it doesn't come from people.

It comes from God Himself.

It is the quiet reassurance that we are not alone.

The stillness that settles beneath the storm.

The voice that reminds us,

"I see your pain, and I'm here with you in it."

This is the kind of comfort that doesn't just make leaders feel better—

It makes them whole.

This is how the Jesus Way strengthens us.

Not by denying the sorrow,

But by redeeming it.

THE SHIFT THAT CHANGES LEADERSHIP

The world says: Great leaders hide their struggles.

Jesus says: **Great leaders bring their struggles to God.**

The world says: Lead from control.

Jesus says: **Lead from surrender.**

The world says: Push past pain.

Jesus says: **Walk through pain with God.**

Leaders who mourn with God are not weaker than others.

They are unshakable.

They are not led by fear. They are led by faith.

This is the Jesus Way.

THE POWER OF MOURNING WITH GOD

Mourning is not the end.

It is a doorway to something greater.

Jesus does not tell us to ignore pain.

He tells us to bring it to God.

Leaders who embrace this truth are not defeated by hardships.

They grow through them.

Because the promise remains:

"Blessed are those who mourn, for they will be comforted."

And that comfort changes everything.

CHAPTER THREE

NEVER LOSE YOUR STRUT

"Blessed are the meek,
for they will inherit the earth."
MATTHEW 5:5

DEFINING MEEKNESS

Meekness is one of those words that doesn't sit well with most people.

It sounds too soft, too submissive—

Too much like stepping aside and letting life walk all over you.

No one wants to be ignored, overlooked, or taken advantage of.

The world rewards those who push forward, take control, and make things happen.

The loudest voices get heard.

The strongest fighters win.

The boldest leaders rise.

When Jesus said, "Blessed are the meek," it must have sounded just as strange to His audience as it does to us now.

But Jesus wasn't interested in telling people what they wanted to hear.

He was telling them the truth—a truth that goes against everything the world teaches.

Meekness is not about giving up or backing down.

It's about knowing exactly who you are and who God is—and walking in that confidence.

It is the deep understanding that you don't have to grasp, fight, or force your way forward.

The meek don't panic when life doesn't go their way.

They don't chase after things that were never meant for them.

They don't lose themselves trying to prove something to the world.

Meekness is strength.

Not the kind that shouts and demands attention—

But the kind that stands firm and remains unshaken.

It's the quiet confidence that refuses to be pulled into fear, anger, or desperation.

Meekness looks at the storms of life and says,

"I don't have to control this. God is in control, and I trust Him."

And that is why Jesus said the meek will inherit the earth.

They don't have to seize it. They don't have to take it.

What God has for them cannot be taken away.

The world tells us to fight for our place.

Jesus tells us to walk in confidence.

The world tells us to control the outcome.

Jesus tells us to trust Him.

Meekness is not passivity.

It is power under control.

And when we understand that, we stop chasing.

We stop forcing.

We start walking in a kind of peace that cannot be shaken.

POWER DOESN'T MEAN CONTROL

The idea of meekness can make us feel uncomfortable.

Because it goes against everything we've been taught about strength.

Strength is supposed to be about winning, achieving, pushing forward, and taking charge.

The world celebrates those who refuse to back down,

Who fight for what they want,

Who bend circumstances to their will.

We're told that if we don't take control, someone else will.

But Jesus presents a completely different picture of strength.

He tells us that **real power isn't about control. It's about trust.**

The meek don't lack power.

They know exactly what they are capable of.

They simply choose not to misuse their abilities.

They don't force what isn't meant for them.

They don't manipulate outcomes to serve their own desires.

They don't let fear or insecurity push them into decisions they were never meant to make.

Decisions made in panic. In pride. In doubt.

Instead, they trust that God's plan is greater than their own.

Meekness isn't passive.

It's an active, deliberate choice to move forward in faith—

Without needing to control everything along the way.

RESISTING THE URGE TO FORCE THINGS

One of the hardest parts of meekness is learning to wait on God instead of rushing ahead.

The urge to step in, fix things, and make something happen is strong.

But where does that urge come from?

For many of us, it comes from fear.

We fear that if we don't act now, we'll miss out.

We fear that if we don't speak up, we'll be forgotten.

We fear that if we don't take control, everything will fall apart.

This fear convinces us that God is slow. That He's forgotten us. That maybe He needs our help.

So we push.

We grasp.

We force.

Others of us don't force things out of fear.

We force things because we have an unhealthy view of our own abilities.

Somewhere along the way, we started believing that success, happiness, and even survival depend entirely on us.

We act as if we are the ones holding everything together.

We convince ourselves that if we don't work harder, push further, or outmaneuver every obstacle, life will never go the way we want.

We may not even realize we think this way, but our constant need for control reveals what we truly believe.

But have you ever noticed that the more you try to force something, the worse it seems to get?

The more we grasp for control, the more life feels chaotic, frustrating, and exhausting.

The moment we let go, the moment we surrender that need, things begin to shift.

That's what meekness does.

It releases us from the constant pressure to figure everything out.

It frees us from the burden of making sure life works exactly the way we think it should.

Instead of constantly fighting, chasing, or proving—

The meek simply walk forward, confident that God is leading them where they need to go.

THE LEADERSHIP STRUT

Meekness is not about waiting for the perfect conditions.

It's about walking forward even when the path is uncomfortable.

It's about moving with confidence—

Not because we have everything figured out

But because we trust the One who does.

The world teaches us that confidence comes from control.

But what happens when life doesn't cooperate?

What happens when the unexpected hits?

When the plan falls apart?

When the path ahead looks anything but clear?

This is where meekness reveals its power.

Meekness is the ability to keep moving, even when the next step isn't obvious.

It's the mindset that says,

"I don't have to control everything to be at peace."

"I don't have to force an outcome to know I'm on the right path."

It is the quiet confidence that allows leaders to remain steady even when everything around them is uncertain.

That's what meekness looks like in real life.

JESUS BEFORE PILATE

He stood before Pilate.

The crowds had cried out for His crucifixion.

The religious leaders demanded answers.

The air was thick with tension—

And yet, Jesus said almost nothing.

Pilate questioned Him.

"Are you the king of the Jews?"

Jesus did not argue.

He did not posture.

He didn't need to defend what was already true.

He answered simply,

"You have said so."

As the accusations flew,

Jesus stood in silence.

He did not fight for His innocence.

He didn't scramble to control the outcome.

Even Pilate was shaken.

"Don't you hear the testimony they are bringing against you?"

But Jesus gave him no reply—not even to a single charge.

The silence was deafening.

Not because it was weak—

But because it was stronger than words.

This is meekness.

Not shrinking back,

Not rolling over,

But standing in surrendered strength—

Knowing that God's plan was still unfolding.

Jesus could have stopped everything.

He could have called down angels.

He could have proven who He was.

But He didn't need to.

Because meekness doesn't grasp.

It trusts.

And even in that courtroom—betrayed, accused, and condemned—

Jesus never lost His strut.

THE QUIET STRENGTH THAT CHANGES EVERYTHING

If you live by the world's definition of strength, you'll always be fighting.

Fighting for control.

Fighting for respect.

Fighting to make things happen.

But if you live with meekness, you'll move through life with unshakable strength.

You'll lead without forcing.

You'll trust without fear.

You'll walk without striving.

And when the rain comes?

You'll keep strutting.

Because you know that God is leading the way.

WHAT DOES "THEY WILL INHERIT THE EARTH" MEAN?

The world tells us to take.

To fight.

To push forward and claim what we think we deserve.

But Jesus promises something radically different.

He doesn't say the meek will conquer the earth.

He says they will inherit it.

An inheritance is not earned through aggression.

It's received through relationship.

This is the quiet reward of meekness.

When you stop striving to take control,

God begins to place things in your hands.

Not because you forced your way to the top—

But because you walked faithfully through the valleys.

To inherit the earth doesn't mean you gain control over people.

It means you receive peace in the places where you live, work, and lead.

You carry influence that heals, not harms.

You shape cultures that reflect heaven, not ego.

The meek don't just receive land.

They inherit impact.

They inherit peace.

They inherit purpose.

They inherit what God has prepared—

And no one can take it from them.

CHOOSING MEEKNESS DAILY

Every day, you will face the choice between:

>   Forcing things or trusting God.

>   Controlling or leading with open hands.

>   Fear or faith.

Meekness isn't a one-time decision.

It's a daily practice.

And when the storm comes?

Keep walking.

Keep trusting.

Keep strutting.

Because no matter what,

God is leading the way.

CHAPTER FOUR

STARVING FOR WHAT'S RIGHT

"Blessed are those who hunger and thirst
for righteousness, for they will be filled."
MATTHEW 5:6

A HUNGER THAT WON'T BE IGNORED

Hunger is not a passing thought. Thirst is not a polite request.

When someone is starving, they do not sit back and hope for food.

They move.

They search.

They pursue.

This is the intensity Jesus is talking about.

"Blessed are those who hunger and thirst for righteousness."

Not "those who like righteousness."

Not "those who agree with righteousness."

Not "those who think righteousness is a good idea."

Jesus is speaking to those who crave righteousness.

Leaders who hunger for righteousness do not wait for goodness to appear.

They are driven to bring it into the world.

They seek it in every decision, every action, every moment.

Most people say they want to do the right thing.

But wanting is not the same as hungering.

A starving person does not wish for food. They chase it.

Leaders who truly hunger for righteousness cannot rest until they see it lived out.

This is what sets righteous leaders apart.

Some leaders hunger for power.

Some hunger for control.

Some hunger for comfort and ease.

But the leaders who hunger for righteousness are different.

They are not satisfied with corruption, dishonesty, or selfish ambition.

They are not content with leadership that serves itself instead of others.

They push forward—not for power or recognition—

But for what is right. Because they must.

This is the heart of the leadership revolution.

It does not begin with strategies or policies.

It begins with hunger.

NOT JUST WANTING—CRAVING

Most people admire righteousness. They respect integrity. They appreciate fairness.

But appreciation is not hunger.

Respect is not thirst.

Jesus is not calling us to simply like righteousness. He is calling us to crave it.

There's a difference.

Many people wish they were in better shape,

But only those who truly hunger for health commit to the process.

They wake up early to train.

They sacrifice.

They push themselves because their bodies demand it.

The same is true of righteousness.

A leader who merely wants to do the right thing will hesitate when it becomes inconvenient.

But a leader who hungers for righteousness will not waver.

Because hunger moves people.

THE COST OF RIGHTEOUSNESS

Righteousness is not free. It costs something.

Sometimes, it will cost approval.

Sometimes, it will cost relationships.

Sometimes, it will cost opportunities.

The world does not always reward integrity.

Sometimes, doing the right thing will make leadership harder.

This is why righteousness must be a hunger, not just a preference.

Leaders who prefer righteousness will let it go when the cost is too high.

Leaders who hunger for righteousness will sacrifice for it.

Because they know it is worth more than approval.

WHAT DOES "FOR THEY WILL BE FILLED" MEAN?

Jesus never calls us to hunger without promising fulfillment.

"Blessed are those who hunger and thirst for righteousness, for they will be filled."

Filled with peace.

Filled with purpose.

Filled with strength.

Filled with clarity.

Most leaders chase success, but success never truly satisfies.

They reach their goals—and still feel empty.

They build their careers—but still long for more.

They win the approval of others—but still battle insecurity.

But the leaders who hunger for righteousness are filled.

They don't chase success only to feel hollow when they arrive.

They are whole.

JESUS AND THE WOMAN AT THE WELL

Some leaders wait for the right moment.

Some wait for the perfect conditions.

Some wait until the crowd is watching.

But leaders who hunger and thirst for righteousness do not wait.

They move.

And that's what Jesus did.

He didn't pursue righteousness when it was easy.

He pursued it when it mattered.

Even when it meant discomfort.

Even when it meant rejection.

Even when it meant taking the long way.

The road through Samaria wasn't necessary.

Most Jewish leaders avoided it—too scandalous, too controversial.

But righteousness doesn't follow the easy road.

It follows calling.

Jesus was tired.

He had been walking all morning.

His throat was dry.

His body ached for rest.

But He kept going.

Because He wasn't just thirsty for water.

He was thirsty for righteousness.

There was someone at the well who needed to be seen.

Someone carrying shame.

Someone hiding from the crowd.

Someone whose heart had gone dry from years of rejection.

She had spent a lifetime chasing the wrong things.

Relationships.

Approval.

Belonging.

But none of it satisfied.

And then—Jesus.

He met her with truth.

He offered her what no one else had:

Living water.

Not rules. Not judgment. Not shame.

But restoration.

He didn't flinch at her past.

He didn't highlight her failures.

He saw her thirst—

And offered her a different kind of fullness.

For the first time, someone looked at her and didn't turn away.

For the first time, someone spoke to her not as an object—

But as a daughter.

And in that moment, righteousness broke through.

Because Jesus didn't just talk about truth—

He brought it near.

She came for water.

But she left with life.

WHAT DRIVES YOU?

Every leader is driven by something.

Some are driven by success.

Some are driven by status.

Some are driven by the need to prove themselves.

Jesus was driven by righteousness.

That's why He went out of His way.

That's why He engaged with people others ignored.

That's why He pursued transformation over tradition.

Leaders who hunger for righteousness do not wait for impact to come to them.

They go after it.

Because righteous leaders lead differently.

WHAT ARE YOU HUNGRY FOR?

Something is stirring inside of you.

Maybe you've been frustrated by leadership that lacks integrity.

Maybe you've seen organizations built on greed instead of goodness.

Maybe you feel called to lead differently.

That's not an accident.

That's the hunger and thirst for righteousness stirring inside you.

Righteous leaders do not lead for power.

They do not lead for applause.

They do not lead for ease.

They lead because they must.

Jesus promised that those who hunger and thirst for righteousness will be filled.

Not with temporary success.

Not with fleeting recognition.

Not with things that fade.

But with peace.

With purpose.

With strength.

With clarity.

The world is filled with leaders who hunger for wealth, recognition, and power.

But the leaders who truly change the world are those who hunger for righteousness.

And if you feel that hunger inside of you, it's time to answer the call.

CHAPTER FIVE

THE HANDS THAT HOLD THE STONES

"Blessed are the merciful,
for they will be shown mercy."
MATTHEW 5:7

WHAT DOES "MERCY" REALLY MEAN?

Mercy is often misunderstood.

Many assume it simply means forgiving others and moving on,

As if it were a passive act of kindness.

But mercy is far more than withholding punishment—

It is an active force that shapes the way we see and respond to people.

Mercy is the choice to meet failure with compassion,

Respond to shortcomings with understanding,

And balance accountability with grace.

Jesus' words,

"Blessed are the merciful, for they will be shown mercy,"

Are not just about offering forgiveness.

They reveal a deeper truth:

The way we treat others will shape the way we are treated.

When we lead with mercy, we create an environment where grace is extended back to us.

This does not mean we ignore wrongdoing or avoid difficult conversations,

But it does mean we seek to build others up rather than tear them down.

Mercy is the ability to see beyond the offense and into the person.

It recognizes that mistakes do not define someone's worth.

It is the choice to respond with wisdom rather than impulse,

With grace rather than condemnation.

Jesus wasn't just saying, "Blessed are those who forgive."

He was saying, "Blessed are those who lead with the same grace they have received."

For leaders, this is a critical mindset shift.

Mercy does not mean a lack of discipline or accountability—

It means discipline that leads to transformation rather than destruction.

When we enforce consequences, we do so not to punish but to help others grow.

Mercy ensures that even in correction, people still feel valued and seen.

THE MINDSET SHIFT FROM JUDGMENT TO UNDERSTANDING

Mercy is not our natural instinct.

When someone wrongs us, fails to meet expectations, or makes a costly mistake,

Our immediate reaction is often frustration, disappointment, or even anger.

The world teaches us that justice means giving people exactly what they deserve.

But what if we've misunderstood what people deserve?

What if justice, in the hands of God, looks more like restoration than revenge?

Mercy challenges the world's mindset.

It calls us to lead differently:

We do not ignore mistakes, but we respond to them in a way that builds rather than breaks.

In this Beatitude, a powerful truth is revealed:

A leader who leads with mercy fosters a culture where grace, patience, and support are extended.

Mercy does not erase consequences,

But it changes the spirit in which those consequences are given.

Instead of reacting with judgment—"They messed up, and they should suffer for it"—

Mercy says, "They messed up, but how can this moment help them grow?"

The old mindset says:

"They made their bed, now they have to lie in it."

"If I go easy on them, they won't learn their lesson."

"Leaders have to be tough—mercy is weakness."

The new mindset says:

"I can hold them accountable while still caring about their growth."

"I won't make decisions out of anger. I'll lead with wisdom and perspective."

"Mercy isn't weakness; it's leadership at its highest level."

WHAT DOES "FOR THEY WILL BE SHOWN MERCY" REALLY MEAN?

At first glance, this part of the verse might seem transactional:

If I show mercy, then I will receive mercy in return.

But the truth goes deeper than that.

Mercy is not a bargaining tool.

It's a reflection of the condition of our hearts.

And when we lead with mercy,

We don't just affect the moment—we shape the mindset of those around us.

Mercy is a force.

It disarms pride, softens tension, and invites others into something better.

It's contagious.

When we show it, others begin to consider it.

And slowly, a culture begins to change.

We align ourselves with God's heart.

We reflect the mercy He has already extended to us.

And there's something else,

Mercy is reciprocal, not because we demand it,

But because people tend to return what they've been given.

A leader who cultivates grace will often be met with grace.

Not because they're perfect,

But because they've modeled what to do when people fall short.

The question isn't whether you'll mess up.

You will.

We all will.

The question is,

When you do, will the people you lead be quick to remember your mercy?

Mercy doesn't lower the bar.

It raises the tone of your leadership.

Mercy is not about lowering standards. It is about elevating leadership.

WHY MERCY IS SO DIFFICULT

Mercy is simple to understand but difficult to practice.

It requires us to override instincts that feel natural—

Frustration, judgment, and even the desire for justice.

We want people to be held accountable, especially when their mistakes affect us.

Mercy asks us to look beyond the offense and see the person, but that's not easy when emotions are involved.

The truth is, judgment is easy.

It gives us a sense of control, a way to categorize people based on their actions.

Someone wrongs us?

We label them untrustworthy.

Someone fails?

We see them as incompetent.

These judgments feel justified in the moment because they protect us.

They allow us to distance ourselves from hurt and frustration.

But mercy challenges us to pause,

Consider the deeper story behind someone's actions,

And choose understanding over condemnation.

This is difficult because it requires humility.

It forces us to acknowledge that we, too, have made mistakes.

We, too, have needed grace.

And sometimes, we don't want to extend grace—

We want people to feel the weight of their failures.

CHRIST SHOWS US A DIFFERENT WAY

The crowd swelled, voices rising in anger.

The woman barely registered the words being hurled at her—
"sinner," "disgrace," "unclean."

Her body ached from being dragged through the streets.

Her knees were scraped raw from the rough stone beneath her.

She could not lift her head. Shame pressed down on her like an unbearable weight.

She knew what was coming. She had seen it before.

A public stoning was not just a punishment; it was a warning to others.

The law was clear. And she had no defense.

A voice cut through the noise.

"Teacher!" one of the religious leaders called out.

"This woman was caught in the act of adultery. In the Law Moses commanded us to stone such women. Now what do you say?"

Silence fell over the crowd as all eyes turned to the man standing in front of them.

Jesus.

He did not respond right away.

Instead, He crouched down, pressing His finger to the dust-covered ground.

The murmuring began again as people whispered and speculated.

What was He doing?

Why wasn't He answering?

The religious leaders smirked, certain they had backed Him into a corner.

Then, He spoke.

"Let any one of you who is without sin be the first to throw a stone at her."

The weight of His words settled over them like a thick fog.

The anger that had fueled the mob flickered, unsteady.

No one moved.

The only sound was the soft scratch of Jesus' finger in the dust.

Then, a dull thud.

A single stone hit the ground.

Then another.

One by one, the men turned and walked away, leaving behind only the woman and Jesus.

She trembled, waiting for the final blow—

The one she had been sure would come.

But instead, she heard His voice again, softer this time.

"Woman, where are they? Has no one condemned you?"

For the first time, she lifted her eyes.

The crowd was gone.

She swallowed hard, barely able to find her voice.

"No one, sir."

Jesus met her gaze, and for the first time in a long time,

She felt seen, not as a sinner, not as a disgrace,

But as a person.

"Then neither do I condemn you," He said. "Go now and leave your life of sin."

This moment was more than just an act of mercy,

It was a lesson in true leadership.

A leader who walks with mercy...

Does not ignore the mistake—

But doesn't make it the whole story either.

They name the truth.

But they speak it with love.

They see the person,

Even when others only see the failure.

They uphold accountability—

Not with anger,

But with peace.

They create space for growth,

Even in the middle of the mess.

They remember what it feels like to need mercy.

And they lead from that place.

They don't shame.

They don't control.

They don't punish to prove a point.

They offer grace with open hands,

Even when letting go is the expected choice.

Because they know—

Mercy doesn't weaken leadership.

It deepens it.

MERCY IS LEADERSHIP AT ITS HIGHEST LEVEL

Leadership isn't just about managing people, it's about developing them.

When you lead with mercy, you create an environment where people feel safe to grow,

Take responsibility, and become better.

Mercy is not weakness, it is leadership at its highest level.

As you step into your next leadership moment, ask yourself:

"Am I leading in a way that helps people grow, or am I reacting based on my emotions?"

"Am I holding people accountable in a way that refines them or just reprimands them?"

"Would I want to be led the way I am leading others right now?"

The world is full of leaders who rule with judgment.

But history remembers the leaders who led with mercy.

MERCY DEFINES YOUR LEADERSHIP LEGACY

At the end of your leadership journey,

People won't just remember the goals you achieved,

The decisions you made, or the policies you enforced.

They will remember how you made them feel in their moments of failure.

Jesus said, "Blessed are the merciful, for they will be shown mercy."

The leaders who live by this principle are the ones who shape lives, not just lead teams.

They build trust, not fear.

They cultivate loyalty, not resentment.

They create environments of transformation rather than cultures of condemnation.

Leadership is not about how many rules you enforce.

It's about how many people you lift up.

Every leader will face moments where they must decide

How to respond to failure, mistakes, and shortcomings.

In those moments, you have a choice:

You can judge quickly, condemn easily, and leave people feeling broken.

Or you can correct wisely, lead patiently, and leave people stronger than you found them.

CHAPTER SIX

CHASING ONE THING

"Blessed are the pure in heart,
for they will see God."
MATTHEW 5:8

MORE THAN MORALITY

When we hear the words "pure in heart,"

We might think of someone who always does the right thing—

Someone who avoids sin, makes good choices, and lives a clean life.

But Jesus was pointing to something deeper.

Purity of heart isn't just about behavior.

It's about focus.

It's about what drives us, what we chase, and why we do the things we do.

Jesus wasn't saying, "Blessed are those who never mess up."

He was saying, "Blessed are those whose hearts are fully devoted to God."

A pure heart isn't a perfect heart—it's an undivided heart.

It's a heart free from competing desires.

A heart that isn't pulled in different directions by ambition, fear, or approval.

A heart that chases one thing—God.

THE DIVIDED HEART

Every one of us feels the pull.

The world teaches us to chase everything at once—success, recognition, comfort, security.

We grow up believing that if we just achieve enough, we'll feel whole.

But no matter how much we accomplish, it's never enough.

We tell ourselves we're following God. But if we're honest?

We're also chasing status.

We're also chasing control.

We're also chasing the need to prove ourselves.

We try to hold on to God with one hand and the world with the other.

But a divided heart will always leave us exhausted.

It's never satisfied.

It always whispers, "Just a little more."

And no matter how much we get, emptiness remains.

THE CALL TO CLARITY

To be pure in heart is to have a clear heart.

A heart not clouded by selfish ambition.

A heart not cluttered by distractions.

A heart fully aligned with God.

This doesn't mean we stop striving or lose ambition.

It means we surrender our ambition to God.

It means we trust Him to lead us where we need to go—

At the right time, in the right way.

But getting there requires honesty.

We have to ask:

"Why am I really doing this?"

"Am I leading to serve God, or am I leading to prove something to myself?"

"Am I chasing my calling, or am I chasing recognition?"

The moment we start asking those questions,

We begin to uncover the real condition of our hearts.

THE POWER OF A PURE-HEARTED LEADER

Leaders with pure hearts don't lead for applause.

They don't need the spotlight.

They don't need external validation.

They are not manipulated by power or controlled by fear.

They lead with clarity.

They don't have to grasp for control—they trust God is directing their steps.

They don't have to fight for position—they know God has already placed them where they need to be.

They don't have to prove their worth—they know their value is already settled.

These are the leaders people trust.

Because they aren't in it for themselves.

Because they don't manipulate, deceive, or chase influence.

Because they don't build their leadership on personal ambition—they build it on calling.

And when a leader knows they are called, they become unstoppable.

WHEN YOUR HEART WANTS BOTH

Most of us want to follow God.

We want to live with purpose.

We want to make a difference.

We want to lead in a way that matters.

But if we're honest?

We also want success.

We also want recognition.

We also want to feel important.

And deep down, we believe we can have both.

We tell ourselves, "As long as I'm doing good things, does it really matter why I'm doing them?"

But Jesus challenges us to think differently.

A pure heart does not want both.

It wants one thing.

It has surrendered everything that competes with God's will.

It doesn't mean we can't have success.

It doesn't mean we can't be recognized.

It just means we don't chase those things.

A divided heart is exhausting.

It keeps us running in circles—

Constantly striving, constantly searching, constantly needing more.

But when our hearts are fully devoted to God?

We stop chasing.

We stop living as if we have something to prove.

We walk in peace.

Because we are no longer pulled in two directions.

JESUS AND THE RICH YOUNG RULER

There is a kind of leader the world admires.

They have all the markers of success—wealth, influence, intelligence, and status.

They've done everything right.

But still, something is missing.

That's the kind of man who came to Jesus one day.

He had everything.

Yet somehow, he still felt incomplete.

He was searching for more.

And he thought Jesus would tell him how to get it.

A QUESTION THAT CHANGED EVERYTHING

The young man moved through the crowd with purpose.

He was used to getting answers.

Used to achieving.

Used to winning.

When he reached Jesus, he knelt—a sign of both respect and urgency.

"Good teacher, what must I do to inherit eternal life?"

Jesus looked at him, recognizing exactly the kind of man he was.

Someone who had lived a good life. Someone who had followed the rules.

"You know the commandments," Jesus replied.

"All these I have kept since I was a boy," the young man said eagerly.

He was expecting affirmation.

Expecting to be told, "You've done enough."

But Jesus saw beyond his words.

He saw his divided heart—the part of him that clung to something other than God.

Mark's Gospel says Jesus looked at him and loved him.

Then He said:

"One thing you lack. Go, sell everything you have and give to the poor, and you will have treasure in heaven. Then come, follow me."

The words hit like a blow.

The young man's face fell.

This was too much.

He had worked too hard. Built too much. Risked too much.

And he wasn't ready to let it go.

Without another word, he turned and walked away.

The young man was good.

But his heart was divided.

He wanted God, but he also wanted control.

Jesus wasn't trying to take everything from him.

He was trying to free him from what was holding him back.

But the young man chose control over calling.

He chose blindness over clarity.

He walked away still searching, still restless, still incomplete.

THE LEADERS WHO SEE GOD

Jesus said, "Blessed are the pure in heart, for they will see God."

Not just in eternity.

Not just in heaven someday.

Here.

Now.

In their leadership. In their decisions. In their daily lives.

A divided heart clouds our vision.

We wonder, "Where is God? Why can't I see Him in my decisions? Why do I feel uncertain?"

But a pure heart sees God everywhere.

A leader with a divided heart asks, "Where is God?"

A leader with a pure heart says, "I see Him everywhere."

This is the blessing of purity of heart.

The blessing of clarity.

The blessing of confidence.

And the blessing of never having to chase what God has already secured.

So ask yourself—"What am I still holding on to?"

Are you ready to let it go?

CHAPTER SEVEN

THE PRESENCE IN THE STORM

"Blessed are the peacemakers,
for they will be called children of God."

MATTHEW 5:9

WHAT DOES IT REALLY MEAN TO BE A PEACEMAKER?

A peacemaker is not just someone who avoids conflict.

Peacemakers are not passive.

They do not walk through life sidestepping tension or pretending everything is fine when it isn't.

A peacemaker is a stabilizing force.

Their presence alone shifts the atmosphere.

They step into chaos with calm.

They step into division with wisdom.

They don't just wish for peace—they create it.

Jesus did not say, "Blessed are those who have no conflict."

He said, "Blessed are the peacemakers."

This means peacemakers are active.

They don't mirror the emotions of the moment—they set the tone.

They do not fuel division, nor do they run from difficult situations.

They engage, but they engage differently.

Peacemakers do not fight fire with fire.

They carry the water of wisdom, patience, and understanding.

Peacemakers are defined by what they bring into the room.

> Do we bring tension or peace?

> Do we bring division or unity?

> Do we escalate problems or work toward resolution?

Jesus was the ultimate peacemaker.

Not because He avoided conflict.

But because He stepped into it with power, purpose, and clarity.

If we want to be peacemakers, we must first cultivate that same peace within ourselves.

FROM REACTING TO LEADING WITH PEACE

Being a peacemaker is not about suppressing emotions or ignoring reality.

It's about mastering your response.

The world teaches us to react.

To meet hostility with hostility.

To match the energy of those who oppose us.

But Jesus calls us to something greater.

A peacemaker is not controlled by external chaos but is led by internal peace.

This requires a radical shift in mindset.

The old mindset reacts to conflict, saying:

"I have to defend myself."

"If someone disrespects me, I'll match their energy."

"If life is chaotic, I have no choice but to be chaotic too."

The new mindset brings peace, saying:

"I don't have to mirror chaos—I can bring peace into any situation."

"I can speak with clarity, not aggression."

"I can step into tension without losing my composure."

The difference is internal strength.

Peacemakers aren't weak—they are anchored.

They are not easily shaken by words, moods, or circumstances.

They understand that control over one's own spirit is the greatest strength a person can possess.

This is what sets peacemakers apart in leadership.

A leader who mirrors chaos only creates more chaos.

But a leader who carries peace becomes a steadying force:

The person others look to when the world feels unstable.

Not because they demand respect—

But because their presence settles the storm.

JESUS CALMING THE STORM

Some moments in Scripture demand that we stop and truly immerse ourselves in them.

The story of Jesus calming the storm is one of those moments.

It is not just an account of a miracle—

It is a master class in what it means to be a peacemaker.

In this scene, we don't just see Jesus teaching about peace—

We see Him embodying it.

While the disciples panic, Jesus rests.

While the storm rages, His faith remains steady.

And when the moment comes, He does not fear the storm.

He does not fight the storm.

He speaks.

And the storm obeys.

This is peacemaking in action.

It's not about avoiding storms.

It's about walking through them with unshakable trust in God's presence and power.

THE STORM AND THE SLEEPER

The wind howled across the sea, turning gentle waves into walls of water.

Rain lashed against the boat.

The disciples fought the storm with everything they had.

Peter gripped the ropes, his muscles burning as he battled against the sea.

His breath came in ragged gasps.

But then—he saw Him.

Jesus.

Asleep.

With the sky splitting open above them, the sea raging, and death inches away—

He was sleeping.

Peter scrambled toward Him, shaking Him violently.

"Teacher, don't you care if we drown?"

Jesus stirred.

His eyes opened slowly, as if waking from a peaceful afternoon nap—

Not a life-threatening storm.

He sat up.

Rubbed the sleep from His face.

Then stood.

The boat lurched violently.

Peter braced himself, expecting Jesus to grab a rope—

To help steady the boat.

But He didn't.

Instead, He stepped forward, lifting a hand toward the storm—

As if greeting an old friend.

The wind shrieked in defiance.

The waves raged.

Jesus exhaled.

Then, in a voice filled with authority, He spoke.

"Quiet! Be still!"

And just like that—

Everything stopped.

The wind silenced.

The waves calmed.

The storm that had threatened to take their lives only moments before,

Was now nothing more than a whisper.

Jesus turned, His gaze sweeping over the disciples.

He met Peter's eyes.

His voice was calm.

"Why are you so afraid? Do you still have no faith?"

The disciples stood in stunned silence.

Their hearts still pounding.

Not from fear of the storm—

But from fear of the One who had just commanded the sea to obey Him.

LESSONS FROM THE STORM

Peacemakers don't just bring peace—

They carry peace within them.

Jesus wasn't calm because the situation was safe—

He was calm because His trust in God was unshakable.

This is the core of being a peacemaker.

Peace isn't about controlling external circumstances.

It's about mastering internal ones.

Peacemakers don't wait for the storm to pass.

They walk in peace through it.

The world panics,

But a peacemaker stands firm.

WHAT DOES "THEY WILL BE CALLED CHILDREN OF GOD" MEAN?

This is not just a reward—

It's a revelation.

To be called a child of God

Is to carry His likeness.

To reflect His presence.

To step into the chaos of the world

And respond the way He would.

Children often carry the spirit of their parents.

They walk like them.

They sound like them.

They remind others of where they came from.

So when Jesus says,

"They will be called children of God,"

He is saying:

When people see how you lead through conflict,

How you step into pain,

How you bring peace without fear—

They'll see God in you.

Not because you're perfect—

But because your presence reminds them of His.

Peacemakers don't just resolve tension.

They reveal the Father.

THE BLESSING OF BEING A PEACEMAKER

This is an active calling.

You are not meant to sit on the sidelines.

You are meant to step into difficult spaces—

With courage, wisdom, and faith.

You are meant to bring clarity where there is confusion.

Healing where there is hurt.

Calm where there is tension.

And in doing so,

You reflect the very heart of God.

You are not just another leader.

You are a peacemaker.

You are a child of God.

CHAPTER EIGHT

THE CROSS WE CARRY

"Blessed are those who are persecuted because of righteousness, for theirs is the kingdom of heaven."
MATTHEW 5:10

WHAT DOES "PERSECUTED BECAUSE OF RIGHTEOUSNESS" REALLY MEAN?

When people hear the word "persecution," they often think of extreme cases—

Believers imprisoned for their faith, executed for refusing to deny Christ,

Or suffering violence because of their beliefs.

And while these forms of persecution are real and still happen today,

Jesus' words in this Beatitude are not limited to the extremes.

Persecution for righteousness takes many forms.

It can be as subtle as being ridiculed or dismissed for standing firm in your values.

It can look like losing relationships because of your faith,

Facing rejection for speaking truth,

Or being attacked for leading with integrity.

When you truly follow Jesus, people will take issue with it.

When you lead with the mindset He set forth, there will be pushback.

This Beatitude is meant to prepare us.

Jesus is not simply saying, "Bad things will happen to you."

He is inviting us to develop a mindset that allows us to face opposition with confidence,

Not fear.

We are not just called to endure persecution—we are called to understand it.

To see it for what it really is.

To recognize the blessing within it.

PERSECUTION IN LEADERSHIP

Leaders who stand for righteousness will face resistance.

Not always in the form of attack—

But in rejection, silence, or subtle isolation.

When a leader refuses to cut corners,

They may be seen as rigid.

When they won't gossip or play favorites,

They may be seen as distant.

When they demand honesty,

They may be pushed aside in favor of someone more "agreeable."

But integrity is not stubbornness.

It is steadfastness.

It is knowing that your character is worth more than temporary approval.

When a leader speaks truth,

They may be labeled divisive—

Even if their words come from love.

Because truth is uncomfortable.

It exposes. It convicts.

And many will resist it

Not because it isn't true—

But because accepting it means they would have to change.

Jesus never avoided truth to keep the peace.

He knew peace without righteousness isn't peace at all.

It's just quiet compromise.

When a leader challenges the status quo,

They will face pushback.

Systems resist disruption.

Comfort clings to tradition.

And those who benefit from the way things are

Will rarely welcome the way things could be.

But leadership isn't about keeping everyone comfortable.

It's about moving forward in obedience—

Even when others don't see the vision yet.

Persecution is not evidence of failure.

It is often the clearest evidence of faithfulness.

If people resist you for doing what is right,

You are likely walking the exact path God intended.

FROM FEAR OF OPPOSITION TO CONFIDENCE IN PURPOSE

When opposition comes, our natural instinct is to question ourselves.

We wonder if we should soften our stance,

Avoid confrontation,

Or adjust our message to be more accepted.

The fear of rejection is real.

But Jesus calls us to a different mindset.

This Beatitude is not just a statement about what will happen—

It is an invitation to prepare our hearts so that when persecution comes,

We are not shaken by it.

We are not called to avoid opposition.

We are called to walk through it with confidence.

The old mindset (fear of rejection), says:

"If I face opposition, I must be doing something wrong."

"Maybe I should stay quiet to keep the peace."

"Maybe I should adjust my message so people don't feel uncomfortable."

"Maybe I misheard God—if this were His will, wouldn't it be easier?"

But Jesus never taught that righteousness would lead to ease.

He taught that righteousness would lead to opposition—

And that this opposition would be a sign we are walking in truth.

The new mindset (confidence in God's plan), says:

"Opposition confirms I am walking in righteousness."

Jesus said, "If the world hates you, keep in mind that it hated me first" (John 15:18).

Rejection from the world is not a sign of failure—

It is evidence that you belong to something greater.

When we stand for truth, we will be resisted by those who benefit from falsehood.

When we lead with righteousness, we will make those who thrive in corruption uncomfortable.

When we refuse to compromise, we will be labeled as the problem.

This is why Jesus doesn't just warn us—He equips us.

He gives us a mindset that sees persecution for what it really is:

A confirmation, not a condemnation.

WHAT DOES "FOR THEIRS IS THE KINGDOM OF HEAVEN" MEAN?

Jesus doesn't just say, "Blessed are those who are persecuted."

He gives us a promise: "For theirs is the kingdom of heaven."

This means:

Persecution is not just the loss of approval—it is the gain of something greater.

The world may reject you, but you already belong to a kingdom that cannot be shaken.

The cost of righteousness is real, but the reward of righteousness is eternal.

When we develop this mindset, persecution no longer has power over us.

It does not define us, defeat us, or change our course.

Instead, it becomes confirmation that we are exactly where we are meant to be.

THIS IS THE COST

Leadership the Jesus Way will not always be applauded.

It will not always be accepted.

It will not always be understood.

There will be moments when you are mocked for your kindness.

Judged for your mercy.

Excluded for your convictions.

And rejected for your compassion.

This is the cost of righteousness.

And it is a cost every leader must face.

To follow Jesus is to carry a cross.

To lead like Jesus is to carry it in front of others—

Publicly.

Boldly.

Willingly.

Jesus never said the road would be easy.

He said it would be worth it.

Because on the other side of persecution is something far greater—

The kingdom of heaven.

But make no mistake:

This Beatitude is not just a promise of reward.

It is a warning.

You will be persecuted if you live this way.

And Jesus did not ask us to do anything He wasn't willing to do first.

A WALK THROUGH REJECTION

Let's go there now—

To the place where Jesus carried His cross.

Not in metaphor.

But in blood and pain and reality.

The time has come.

He has been arrested.

Beaten.

Mocked.

Judged.

Abandoned.

The crowd is restless—

Their chants no longer sing His name.

Their eyes are cold.

Their fists are tight.

He stands in silence.

A robe stained with blood clings to His back.

A crown of thorns presses deep into His brow.

And the cross—

Rough, splintered, heavy—

Is dropped onto His shoulders.

The wood carves into flesh.

Each step presses agony into His spine.

He stumbles.

He gasps.

He bleeds.

He does not turn back.

The same hands that healed the blind…

Now cling to the dust for balance.

The same voice that calmed the storm…

Now breathes through pain.

He walks forward—

Not just to His death,

But to our salvation.

And in this brutal, heart-wrenching moment,

We find a leader like no other.

He does not fight back.

He does not call down angels.

He does not trade insult for insult.

He carries the weight.

He walks the road.

He endures the pain.

Because righteousness is not just something He taught—

It is something He lived.

This is what it means to lead the Jesus Way.

OUR OWN CROSSES

You may never carry a physical cross.

You may never be beaten for your beliefs.

But make no mistake:

Persecution still comes.

You may be judged.

Overlooked.

Excluded.

Mocked.

Dismissed.

Not because of poor performance—

But because of righteousness.

The world is not always kind to those who walk in truth.

Because truth convicts.

Truth disrupts.

Truth doesn't play by the rules of ego, power, or control.

And when you choose to lead with humility, mercy, and conviction—

You will be different.

And when you are different,

You will be noticed.

Not always in the way you hoped.

But you are blessed.

Blessed are the leaders who stand firm in grace.

Who refuse to fight hate with hate.

Who let their light shine in the dark—

Even when the darkness fights back.

HOW DO WE RESPOND?

We do not match hate with hate.

We do not let fear make us small.

We do not twist righteousness into self-righteousness.

We do not become arrogant defenders of truth.

We lead in love.

We walk in truth.

We carry the cross with humility and courage.

We show the world what it looks like to live with peace even when attacked.

To lead with integrity even when questioned.

To respond with compassion even when rejected.

Because leadership the Jesus Way is not reactive.

It is resilient.

It is rooted.

It is righteous.

A FINAL WORD TO THE PERSECUTED LEADER

If you've been misunderstood—

If you've been judged for doing the right thing—

If you've been excluded because of your integrity—

You are not failing.

You are following.

You are walking the same path Jesus walked.

And though it hurts—

Though it costs you something—

It is not in vain.

For yours is the kingdom of heaven.

Not just someday.

But even now.

Every time you choose obedience over approval—

You step further into that kingdom.

Every time you choose grace over retaliation—

You bring that kingdom to earth.

The cross you carry is not a symbol of defeat.

It is a sign of partnership.

A sign that you walk with Jesus.

That He walks with you.

And that through your leadership,

Heaven touches earth.

THE REWARDS
OF LEADERSHIP

CHAPTER NINE

A DIFFERENT KIND OF SUCCESS

*"I have come that they may have
life, and have it to the full."*

JOHN 10:10

THE REWARDS OF A RENEWED MIND

Leadership has always been about results.

From the boardroom to the battlefield, from the pulpit to the production floor—

Leaders are measured by what they produce.

Profits.

Power.

Influence.

Impact.

We're taught that success belongs to those who work harder, climb higher,

And push further than everyone else.

And yet—how many leaders reach the top only to feel empty when they get there?

How many spend years sacrificing everything—health, family, peace of mind—

In pursuit of a reward that never truly satisfies?

The world rewards leadership one way. But Jesus offers something far better.

The first half of this book has been about the mindset of a leader who follows the Jesus Way.

We've explored how Jesus calls us to lead with humility, meekness, mercy, and righteousness.

How leadership is a daily practice—

Of putting pride to death daily, resisting the temptation of control,

And trusting God's timing over our own.

It is not the easiest path.

But it is the only one that leads to true fulfillment.

Now, we shift our focus to what this kind of leadership gives in return.

We've explored each Beatitude—each mindset Jesus called us to adopt.

But in this section, we step into something different.

We're not just focused on the way of thinking.

We're focused on what that way of thinking produces.

These are the rewards Jesus spoke about—

Not just in Matthew but throughout His life and ministry.

This section is about new rewards.

The kind that cannot be taken away.

The kind that don't disappear when the economy shifts or the applause fades.

Peace.

Joy.

Purpose.

Legacy.

These are the rewards Jesus promised.

The rewards that come from leading with a heart aligned to Him.

This isn't about rejecting results or ignoring success.

Metrics matter.

We cannot lead if we don't produce.

But the challenge is this:

Will success own us, or will we own success?

Will we lead only to please the business?

Or will we lead in a way that makes us whole?

The world measures leadership by how much you gain.

The Jesus Way measures leadership by who you become.

And when you lead this way, you will gain far more than you ever imagined.

THE ILLUSION OF SUCCESS

At some point, almost every leader has been sold the same promise:

Work hard.

Climb the ladder.

Outthink the competition.

Eventually, you'll reach the top.

You'll have wealth, influence, admiration—proof that you've made it.

The world calls this success.

And yet—how many leaders get there only to feel an unsettling truth creeping in?

They have the title.

They have the money.

They have the power.

But somehow… it's still not enough.

The exhaustion from years of striving won't fade.

The weight of decisions that don't align with their values lingers.

The applause doesn't last as long as it used to.

And the quiet voice inside asks:

"Is this really all there is?"

Leadership—when pursued for the wrong rewards—becomes a race with no finish line.

THE OLD REWARDS OF LEADERSHIP

For centuries, leadership has been measured by what can be seen.

Financial gain.

Leadership often comes with perks—

Bonuses, stock options, paychecks that reward performance.

And while money matters, when it becomes the measure of success, no amount is ever "enough."

Power and control.

Influence is a part of leadership.

But power is addictive.

The tighter we grip it, the more isolated we become—

Leading from fear rather than freedom.

Recognition and status.

The applause. The title. The award.

These can validate hard work,

But when recognition becomes the goal, leaders start making decisions to be liked...

Not to do what's right.

Winning at all costs.

Competition can fuel growth—

But it can also turn toxic.

When the race becomes about proving others wrong,

We forget why we were running in the first place.

These old rewards aren't evil.

But when they become the reason we lead,

They leave us empty—

Chasing a finish line that never satisfies.

THE STORY OF BOB CHAPMAN

Few leaders have achieved business success and personal transformation like Bob Chapman, CEO of Barry-Wehmiller.

Early in his career, Chapman embodied the traditional CEO.

Focused on profitability, efficiency, and expansion, he made strategic acquisitions and turned struggling companies around.

By every traditional metric, he was winning.

His company was growing.

His wealth was increasing.

His leadership was respected.

But something was wrong.

Despite Barry-Wehmiller's success, Chapman noticed something troubling.

His employees didn't seem fulfilled.

They weren't thriving—they were enduring.

Work wasn't a place of purpose. It was a paycheck.

Then, something changed.

One day, at a wedding, Chapman watched a father walk his daughter down the aisle.

And suddenly, it hit him:

Every employee is someone's son or daughter.

Someone's precious child—entrusted to his care.

That moment shattered his view of leadership.

And he changed the way he led.

Instead of focusing solely on numbers, he started focusing on people.

He restructured Barry-Wehmiller's leadership model to put employees first—

Prioritizing trust, empathy, and shared purpose.

What happened next defied expectations.

Instead of losing ground, Barry-Wehmiller grew exponentially:

> The company went from twenty million to three billion in revenue—with 20 percent annual growth over two decades.

> Barry-Wehmiller completed more than one hundred successful acquisitions—turning struggling businesses into thriving ones.

But the greatest transformation wasn't in profits—it was in people.

> Employee well-being soared. Job satisfaction and personal fulfillment increased.

Relationships improved. A culture of care spilled over into families and communities.

Growth skyrocketed. Employees felt valued, respected, and empowered.

Chapman's journey proves something profound:

True leadership isn't about chasing power, money, or status.

It's about valuing people.

And that is the Jesus Way.

WHAT ARE YOU CHASING?

Every leader must ask themselves:

"What am I really chasing?"

"Am I leading to please the business or to build something that truly lasts?"

"Am I working for applause or for impact?"

"Am I striving for power or for purpose?"

If the old rewards of leadership leave you unsatisfied…

Maybe it's because you were meant for something greater.

And that's what we're about to explore next.

CHAPTER TEN

THE REWARD OF PEACE

*"In this world you will have trouble. But
take heart! I have overcome the world."*

JOHN 16:33

THE BURDEN OF LEADERSHIP WITHOUT PEACE

Imagine this:

You wake up before the sun, your mind already racing.

The day ahead is packed.

Your inbox is overflowing, deadlines loom,

And a meeting later in the afternoon could change everything.

You haven't had a real day off in weeks—

Stepping away feels impossible.

There's always one more email, one more crisis, one more decision
only you can make.

At night, you lie in bed staring at the ceiling, exhausted but unable to rest.

The stress lingers in your chest like a weight that never lifts.

The moment you put one fire out, another one flares up.

The demands never stop, and neither does your mind.

This is leadership without peace.

Always carrying.

Always grinding.

Never resting.

The world tells us this is normal—

That stress is just part of leadership.

That the burden is proof of our importance.

But what if it's not supposed to be this way?

What if leadership could feel lighter?

What if you could lead powerfully and effectively without being consumed by anxiety?

What if you could experience peace even in the middle of pressure?

Jesus promised a different way.

THE PEACE THAT COMES FROM THE JESUS WAY

Jesus led under constant pressure.

Crowds followed Him everywhere.

Religious leaders plotted against Him.

His disciples misunderstood Him.

Yet, through it all…

He walked in peace.

> When a violent storm raged around Him, He slept in the boat.
>
> When falsely accused, He remained composed.
>
> When facing the cross, He trusted the Father's plan.

This kind of peace isn't about escaping leadership challenges.

It's about leading with a different spirit.

Jesus didn't lead with anxious striving. He led with divine assurance.

He knew who He was.

He knew who He served.

He knew who was in control.

And because of that, He never led from fear.

EXPERIENCING THE REWARD OF PEACE

Close your eyes for a moment and imagine yourself leading this way.

Imagine waking up without the crushing weight of pressure on your chest.

Imagine moving through the day with confidence instead of worry.

Imagine stepping into high-stakes meetings or hard conversations without anxiety ruling you.

What if your mind was clear, your spirit was steady, and your heart was at peace—

No matter what challenges came your way?

This is the reward of peace that Jesus offers.

> Not peace that depends on circumstances.

> Not peace that only comes when everything is going right.

> But peace that remains—even when the storm rages.

WHAT TRUE PEACE LOOKS LIKE

Most people think of peace as a destination—a moment when everything finally settles.

The world defines peace as:

> The absence of conflict.

The removal of stress.

The resolution of every problem.

But this definition makes peace fragile.

It means peace is always just out of reach—because there's always another problem.

But the peace Jesus offers?

It's something entirely different.

Jesus never promised a storm-free life.

In fact, He told His disciples,

"In this world you will have trouble. But take heart! I have overcome the world."

His promise wasn't a life free from stress but peace amid the pressure.

THE WORLD'S PEACE VS. JESUS' PEACE

The world offers peace that's conditional—

Peace that depends on the absence of conflict,

On calm surroundings,

On everything going according to plan.

But Jesus offers peace that holds steady in the chaos—

Peace that endures through the storm.

Not because the storm disappears,

But because God's presence never does.

The world's peace is external—

Shaped by people, pressure, and performance.

But Jesus' peace is internal—

Anchored in trust.

Rooted in truth.

Unshakable.

WHY LEADERS STRUGGLE TO FIND PEACE

If Jesus offers us peace, why do so many leaders live without it?

Why do we accept stress as "part of the job" instead of embracing the peace we were promised?

Because the greatest threat to peace isn't external pressure—it's internal resistance.

We block the peace God offers because we've been conditioned to believe peace must be earned.

Some leaders never find peace—

Not because they don't want it,

But because they're chasing the wrong version of it.

They confuse peace with control.

They think if they can manage every outcome,

Or predict every variable,

Then peace will follow.

But control is not peace.

It's worry wearing a mask.

They confuse peace with perfection.

They believe that once the problems go away,

Once the chaos settles,

Once they're better, stronger, more capable…

Then they'll finally rest.

But perfection is a mirage.

True peace doesn't wait for circumstances to align—

It enters the mess with grace.

And some confuse peace with escape.

They withdraw.

They disconnect.

They shrink from hard conversations,

Thinking avoidance will bring relief.

But peace doesn't come from distance.

It comes from presence.

From courage.

From walking through—not around—the storm.

HOW TO LEAD WITH PEACE

You start by remembering who you walk with.

Peace isn't something you create—

It's something you receive.

You pause before the panic.

You breathe before the battle.

You speak to God before you speak to the problem.

The world trains leaders to solve every issue immediately.

But Jesus trained His followers to rest—

Even in the middle of the storm.

Peace doesn't mean passivity.

It means presence.

A mind that is still.

A heart that trusts.

A spirit that listens.

This is where peace begins.

CHAPTER ELEVEN

REDISCOVERING THE JOY OF LEADERSHIP

*"I have told you this so that my joy may be in
you and that your joy may be complete."*

JOHN 15:11

WHEN LEADERSHIP BECOMES A BURDEN

Leadership was supposed to be exciting.

It was supposed to be fulfilling.

But for many leaders, it doesn't feel that way anymore.

Somewhere along the journey, the excitement faded.

Leadership became a burden instead of a blessing.

The passion that once fueled you has turned into exhaustion.

The victories feel brief, while the weight of responsibility never lifts.

You wonder…

"Is it possible to enjoy leadership the way I once did?"

Have you ever felt this way?

Like the joy has drained out of leadership?

Like you're carrying a weight instead of walking in purpose?

You're not alone.

Many leaders spend their days feeling drained, disconnected, and weary.

But what if leadership wasn't meant to be a constant grind?

What if joy wasn't occasional but was something you carried daily?

Jesus promised a different way to lead.

A way that isn't fueled by pressure but by joy.

WHAT IS TRUE JOY?

Most people confuse joy with happiness.

Happiness is based on circumstances. It comes and goes.

Joy is deeper. It is steady, unshakable, and doesn't depend on what's happening around you.

Jesus never said, "I will make you happy."

He said, "I have told you this so that my joy may be in you and that your joy may be complete."

Complete joy is:

Not temporary.

Not dependent on external success.

Not something you have to chase.

Joy is a gift.

And when you lead the Jesus Way, it's a reward that comes naturally.

So why do so many leaders struggle to experience it?

WHY LEADERS LOSE THEIR JOY

Leaders don't lose their joy all at once.

It fades slowly—

Buried beneath the weight of pressure,

Expectation,

And the lie that they must hold everything together.

Sometimes, leaders lose their joy

Because they confuse joy with results.

They believe joy comes only when things are going well—

When the team performs,

When the goal is reached,

When the scoreboard says they're winning.

But joy that depends on outcomes isn't joy.

It's approval in disguise.

Sometimes, they lose joy

Because they stop doing what brings it.

They become so consumed with leading others

That they forget to be led themselves.

They stop praying.

They stop creating.

They stop sitting in God's presence

And wonder why they feel empty.

And sometimes, leaders lose their joy

Because they're carrying burdens

They were never meant to carry alone.

They lead from pressure,

Not presence.

From fear,

Not faith.

WHAT LEADING WITH JOY FEELS LIKE

Now, take a moment.

Imagine walking into work with energy and anticipation instead of dread.

Imagine feeling connected to your purpose again.

Imagine laughing more, enjoying your team, celebrating wins—feeling full instead of empty.

Imagine waking up not with pressure but with passion.

Not with burden but with excitement.

What would change if leadership felt life-giving again?

This is the reward of joy.

Not joy that comes and goes.

But joy that remains, even in the hard moments.

This isn't wishful thinking.

This is what Jesus carried.

Let's see how He modeled this kind of leadership.

JESUS LEADING WITH JOY

Jesus' leadership was never meant to stay small.

In addition to His twelve disciples,

He expanded His mission by sending out seventy-two more followers (Luke 10:1–21).

This was a turning point in His leadership—let's take a deeper look.

He had spent years pouring into His followers.

He had taught them, guided them, prepared them.

Now, it was time for them to go out on their own.

Imagine this moment.

Jesus sends them out to heal the sick, cast out demons, and share the kingdom.

They go.

They step out in faith.

And when they return, they are overflowing with joy.

"Lord, even the demons submit to us in your name" (Luke 10:17).

They are energized, excited, alive.

And what does Jesus do?

He celebrates with them.

"At that time Jesus, full of joy through the Holy Spirit, said, 'I praise you, Father, Lord of heaven and earth'" (Luke 10:21).

Did you catch that?

Jesus was full of joy.

He took deep pleasure in seeing those He led step into their calling.

He didn't lead with cynicism, exhaustion, or obligation.

He rejoiced in the growth of His people.

This is the kind of joy we're meant to experience in leadership.

A joy that comes from:

Seeing others grow.

Watching God move.

Leading in a way that isn't draining but is life-giving.

This is the joy of leadership done right.

This is the reward that keeps you going.

This is what the Jesus Way offers.

Imagine leading from joy again.

Feeling reconnected to your purpose.

Leading without the weight of exhaustion.

Waking up excited about what's ahead instead of dreading it.

Joy is not a luxury in leadership—it's a necessity.

Without joy, leadership feels like a burden.

With joy, leadership feels like a calling.

This is what Jesus promised—a joy that is complete, unshaken, and always available.

And when you lead for others' good, joy is no longer something you chase.

It's something you live in.

CHAPTER TWELVE

LEADING WITH CLARITY AND CONVICTION

"'My food,' said Jesus, 'is to do the will of him
who sent me and to finish his work.'"

JOHN 4:34

THE REWARD OF PURPOSE

You reached the goal.

You built the team.

You hit the numbers.

You made it to the top.

And yet... something still feels off.

You should feel satisfied. But instead, you feel disconnected.

Have you ever been there?

Many leaders achieve success only to find it lacking.

They thought the next milestone would fulfill them.

They assumed that once they arrived, they'd feel complete.

But something is missing.

The truth?

We weren't just created to succeed.

We were created to lead with purpose.

And there is no greater reward in leadership than knowing exactly why you are leading.

WHAT IS TRUE PURPOSE?

The world defines purpose by what you do.

It tells you that your purpose is found in:

    Your passion.

    Your work.

    Your achievements.

But purpose isn't just about what you do.

Purpose is about who you serve.

Jesus didn't come searching for His passion—He came to fulfill His mission.

He didn't chase success—He walked in obedience.

That's where true purpose is found.

"My food," said Jesus, "is to do the will of him who sent me and to finish his work."

Jesus compared purpose to food.

It sustains us.

It energizes us.

It gives us life.

That's what makes purpose a reward.

It's not something we achieve once—it's something we receive daily.

The more we walk in it, the more whole we become.

This is why Jesus said His food was to do the will of the Father.

Because purpose fills us. It nourishes us.

It's not just what we pursue.

It's what satisfies us.

True purpose is not found in achievements.

True purpose is found in alignment with God's will.

WHY SO MANY LEADERS STRUGGLE WITH PURPOSE

Some leaders struggle to find purpose—

Not because they don't care,

But because they're looking in the wrong places.

They confuse purpose with position.

They believe that once they have the title,

The influence,

The corner office—

Then they'll feel fulfilled.

But purpose isn't tied to role.

It's tied to impact.

You can lead from anywhere

When you know who you are.

Some leaders confuse purpose with productivity.

They check every box,

Meet every deadline,

Achieve every goal—

But still feel empty.

Because purpose isn't about how much you get done.

It's about why you do it.

They confuse purpose with pressure.

They think if it's hard, it must be important.

If it's stressful, it must be meaningful.

But pressure without clarity

Is just weight.

Purpose may be heavy—

But it's never aimless.

LEADING WITH PURPOSE

A leader with purpose

Knows they were sent—

Not just hired,

Not just promoted,

But positioned.

They don't just lead projects.

They lead people toward wholeness.

They measure success by growth,

Not just results.

They ask hard questions.

They make courageous decisions.

They choose impact over impression.

They don't just want a team that performs.

They want a team that thrives.

Because purpose isn't about what you accomplish—

It's about who becomes stronger because you led.

THE NIGHT BEFORE THE CROSS

It's the final night before His crucifixion.

Jesus knows what's coming.

He knows He will be betrayed.

He knows He will suffer.

He knows the cross is ahead.

Yet instead of panicking… He prays.

This is the moment where leadership and purpose collide.

For three years, Jesus had taught, healed, and led.

He had poured into His disciples, challenged the religious elite,

And revealed the kingdom of God.

But this—this was the purpose He had carried all along.

The cross wasn't a failure in His leadership—it was the fulfillment of it.

The world saw humiliation, but Jesus saw victory.

The world saw an ending, but Jesus saw completion.

The cross was His ultimate purpose statement.

Not power.

Not recognition.

Not earthly success.

But sacrifice. Love. Redemption.

This is what true purpose looks like.

It is not about avoiding hardship—

It is about walking fully in what you were called to do, no matter the cost.

In John 17:4, Jesus said, "I have brought you glory on earth by finishing the work you gave me to do."

Imagine the confidence and clarity it takes to say that.

Jesus doesn't say,

"I did most of what you wanted me to."

"I tried my best."

"I'm still figuring things out."

No. He says with certainty that He finished the work the Father gave Him.

But this confidence wasn't something Jesus found at the finish line—

It was how He led from the very beginning.

Jesus didn't wait until the end to declare His purpose—every step of His journey was intentional.

From calling His disciples to healing the broken, every moment was aligned with His mission.

His clarity didn't start in the final hour—it was present from the very beginning.

This is the ultimate picture of purpose.

Jesus didn't drift.

He didn't get distracted.

He didn't let the expectations of others pull Him away from His calling.

Instead, He led with unshakable purpose.

Now, imagine reaching the end of your leadership journey and being able to say the same.

STEPPING INTO YOUR PURPOSE

Imagine waking up every morning with absolute clarity.

No more wondering if you're in the right place.

No more chasing someone else's definition of success.

No more questioning if your leadership truly matters.

Instead, you wake up with a clear mission.

You know who you are.

You know what you're called to do.

You know that God is guiding every step.

That's the reward of purpose.

And when we lead the Jesus Way…

We don't just lead well.

We lead with certainty.

CHAPTER THIRTEEN

BUILDING SOMETHING THAT LASTS

"Very truly I tell you, whoever believes in me
will do the works I have been doing, and they
will do even greater things than these."
JOHN 14:12

THE REWARD OF LEGACY

Your leadership will outlive you.

The question isn't if you'll leave a legacy.

The question is what kind of legacy you'll leave behind.

Many leaders chase success but never build something meaningful.

They focus on profits, not people.

They build a reputation, not a legacy.

They measure their influence by what they accomplish, not by who they develop.

But the Jesus Way offers a different kind of leadership.

One that multiplies beyond you.

One that doesn't die when you leave.

One that outlives your time, your title, and even your lifetime.

WHAT IS TRUE LEGACY?

The world defines legacy as:

Being remembered.

Leaving behind achievements, wealth, or influence.

Having people look back on your work with admiration.

But Jesus defined legacy differently.

Legacy isn't about being remembered.

Legacy is about multiplying impact beyond yourself.

Jesus never built an empire.

He built people.

And that's why His influence didn't fade—it only grew.

Jesus said, "Very truly I tell you, whoever believes in me will do the works I have been doing, and they will do even greater things than these."

Think about that.

Jesus wasn't obsessed with building a legacy for Himself.

He wasn't chasing reputation.

He didn't need to protect His name—

Because He trusted the Father to glorify Him at the right time, in the right way.

His focus was obedience.

His mission was love.

And His legacy was not crafted—it was revealed through His surrender.

He empowered others to carry the mission forward. Even beyond what He had done.

That's what true leadership does.

It doesn't end when you step away.

It continues through the lives you've invested in.

WHY SOME LEADERS LEAVE NO LASTING IMPACT

Some leaders leave no lasting impact—

Not because they lacked ambition,

But because they led for themselves.

They never led with people in mind.

The goal was achievement, not transformation.

The focus was performance, not development.

They led to prove something—

Not to shape someone.

They led from fear or ego.

They used their role to feel powerful,

Not to make others powerful.

Their presence left pressure—

Not peace.

They didn't pour into others.

They held onto wisdom instead of sharing it.

They managed instead of mentored.

They led alone—

And so their impact ended with them.

HOW TO LEAD WITH LEGACY IN MIND

If you want to leave a legacy—

Don't chase applause.

Don't build monuments.

Don't cling to control.

Lead with people in mind.

See who's in the room—

And what they need most.

Remember: It's not about being remembered.

It's about helping others remember who they are.

Lead with humility.

Not the kind that hides—

But the kind that lifts.

Be honest about your own need for grace,

And generous in how you extend it.

Invest in others.

Pour into the next generation.

Share what you've learned.

Legacy is not what you leave behind—

It's who you've lifted up along the way.

JESUS' LEGACY THROUGH HIS DISCIPLES

Jesus' impact didn't end with Him.

It exploded.

Why?

Because He didn't build an institution.

He built people.

He didn't hoard leadership.

He passed it on.

He didn't lead for His own success.

He led for eternal impact.

Before ascending into heaven, Jesus speaks His final words to His followers:

"All authority in heaven and on earth has been given to me. Therefore go and make disciples of all nations, baptizing them in the name of the Father and of the Son and of the Holy Spirit, and teaching them to obey everything I have commanded you. And surely I am with you always, to the very end of the age" (Matthew 28:18–20).

And then—He leaves.

No safety net.

No backup plan.

Just trust in the ones He trained.

And because of that?

Over two thousand years later, His legacy is still growing.

THE LEADERSHIP DECISION THAT LASTS

Legacy isn't built in the future.

It's built in every decision you make today.

How you invest in people.

How you release control.

How you choose faithfulness over fame.

Success fades. Impact multiplies.

Don't wait until the end of your career to ask, "Did my leadership truly matter?"

Make the decision now to build something that lasts.

Because when you lead the Jesus Way, your leadership never dies.

CHAPTER FOURTEEN

THE TRUE REWARDS OF LEADERSHIP

"Let us not become weary in doing
good, for at the proper time we will reap
a harvest if we do not give up."

GALATIANS 6:9

KEEP MOVING FORWARD

We've now explored four great rewards of leadership.

Peace: Leading without anxiety or pressure.

Joy: Leading with energy and passion again.

Purpose: Leading with clarity, knowing you're aligned with God's calling.

Legacy: Leading in a way that outlives you.

These are not the rewards the world offers.

The world tells leaders to chase:

Money

Power

Status

Recognition

But the Jesus Way offers:

Peace that frees you from fear.

Joy that fuels your leadership.

Purpose that gives you clarity and direction.

Legacy that multiplies your impact beyond your lifetime.

This is what leadership was meant to be.

This is what Jesus promised.

This is the Jesus Way.

A LEADERSHIP SHIFT

Imagine waking up every day knowing:

You don't have to carry the weight alone.

You don't have to chase success to feel fulfilled.

You don't have to fear failure because your purpose is bigger than a single moment.

Instead of striving...

You trust.

Instead of chasing…

You build.

Instead of wondering if your leadership matters…

You lead with confidence, knowing that it does.

And this isn't just an idea.

This is the reward of leading the Jesus Way.

SALT AND LIGHT

CHAPTER FIFTEEN

THE FLAVOR OF LEADERSHIP

*"You are the salt of the earth. But if the salt
loves its saltiness, how can it be made salty
again? It is no longer good for anything, except
to be thrown out and trampled underfoot."*

MATTHEW 5:13

THE TASTE OF LEADERSHIP

Leadership has a flavor.

Every leader leaves a taste in the lives of those they lead.

Some leaders leave behind bitterness.

Their presence is overwhelming, their words cut,

And their leadership feels more like control than guidance.

Some leaders leave behind blandness.

They manage, but they don't inspire;

They keep the system running, but they never enhance anything.

But then there are leaders who leave behind richness, depth, and nourishment.

These leaders make people better, stronger, and more fulfilled.

This is what Jesus was talking about when He said, "You are the salt of the earth. But if the salt loses its saltiness, how can it be made salty again? It is no longer good for anything, except to be thrown out and trampled underfoot."

Salt was a powerful symbol in Jesus' time.

It wasn't just seasoning—it was a preservative, a purifier, and an enhancer.

It was essential for survival.

It made the ordinary extraordinary.

And Jesus says: That's who you are supposed to be.

WHAT KIND OF FLAVOR ARE YOU OFFERING?

Every leader adds a flavor to the people they lead.

This is why Jesus compared us to salt.

Salt isn't just a nice addition—it fundamentally changes the experience of what it touches.

Leadership works the same way.

Great leaders leave people better than they found them.

Weak leaders leave people worse off.

And here's the key:

Salt doesn't try to be sweet.

Salt doesn't try to be something it's not.

Salt embraces its purpose and does what it was designed to do.

This is the foundation of the Jesus Way: **We don't lead like the world does.**

We don't chase power or status to feel valuable.

We don't seek control to prove we're in charge.

We lead through a renewed mind, bringing out the best in others.

And when we lead this way?

We make people hungry for something more.

> A great leader doesn't just make people more productive—they make people better.

> A great leader doesn't just run an organization—they build a movement.

> A great leader doesn't just give orders—they ignite a passion for something greater.

THE DANGER OF DILUTED LEADERSHIP

Jesus' warning is clear:

"If the salt loses its saltiness, how can it be made salty again? It is no longer good for anything, except to be thrown out and trampled underfoot."

This isn't just a general statement, it's a leadership principle.

Think about the leaders you've seen who started strong but lost their way.

The leader who once inspired people… but became focused on power and self-preservation.

The leader who stood for something… but compromised values for money or recognition.

The leader who once cared deeply about people… but let bitterness or burnout steal their heart.

This is what it means to lose saltiness.

It's when a leader:

Stops enhancing—they just go through the motions.

Stops preserving—they let corruption creep in.

Stops creating thirst—they no longer inspire anyone.

And what happens to that kind of leader?

People stop listening. People stop following. People stop trusting.

Jesus says when salt loses its saltiness, it is no longer good for anything.

This doesn't mean a leader is worthless—it means they have lost their ability to truly make an impact.

The world is full of bland, diluted leadership.

The world is full of leaders who blend in rather than stand out.

Jesus is calling us to be different.

To lead with flavor.

To enhance the world.

To bring something that can't be ignored.

And that's where our biblical example comes in.

JESUS AS THE ULTIMATE SALT-FILLED LEADER

The street was loud.

Not with voices of praise—

But with words of disgust.

People didn't speak Levi's name with affection.

They spoke it with contempt.

A traitor.

A thief.

A man who had sold his soul to collect for Rome.

He heard their mutters.

He felt their eyes.

He knew what they thought of him—

And maybe, on most days, he agreed.

But not today.

Because today,

Jesus walked by.

He didn't spit.

He didn't lecture.

He didn't call Levi out.

He called him in.

"Follow me."

No explanation.

No condemnation.

Just an invitation.

And for reasons Levi couldn't explain—

He stood up.

He walked away from the table.

And never looked back.

That night, the house was full.

Laughter echoed off the walls.

The wine flowed.

The food was simple, but the joy was rich.

Levi had gathered the only people who had ever accepted him—

Other tax collectors.

Outcasts.

Sinners.

And now,

Jesus.

He didn't stand in the corner.

He didn't look down His nose.

He reclined at the table.

Comfortable. Present. Unbothered by the shame others saw—

Because He saw something different.

He saw image-bearers.

He saw hunger—

Not for food,

But for love that wasn't transactional.

And His presence made them wonder:

What kind of teacher sits with men like us?

What kind of holy man calls someone like Levi?

What kind of God draws near instead of walking away?

Outside, the Pharisees whispered.

Not to Jesus—

But to His disciples.

"Why does your teacher eat with tax collectors and sinners?"

They didn't understand.

They didn't see the salt.

The preservation of dignity.

The enhancement of worth.

The thirst being stirred for something eternal.

Jesus heard them.

He stood—not with defensiveness,

But with clarity.

"It is not the healthy who need a doctor, but the sick.

I have not come to call the righteous, but sinners."

He didn't apologize for the company He kept.

He didn't soften His mission.

He stood in the middle of the tension

And seasoned the whole moment with grace.

In that house, Jesus didn't just teach salt—

He was salt.

He enhanced what religion had buried.

He preserved the dignity of those the world had discarded.

And He stirred up a thirst for grace that no one else had ever offered.

This is the Jesus Way.

Not distant. Not sanitized.

But present. Flavorful. Unignorable.

And if this is how Jesus led—

This is how we must lead too.

THE FUTURE OF LEADERSHIP NEEDS MORE SALT

Think about the leaders you've encountered in your life.

Some left you drained, discouraged, and defeated.

Some were forgettable and neutral, just keeping the system running.

But some were different.

They challenged you to grow.

They protected what mattered.

They ignited something in you that made you want to do more, be more, and live differently.

That's the kind of leader Jesus calls us to be.

Because when we live as salt-filled leaders, something powerful happens:

Jesus places us where we can have the most impact.

Salt doesn't choose where it lands.

Salt simply brings its flavor wherever it is placed.

CHAPTER SIXTEEN

THE DIRECTION OF LEADERSHIP

"You are the light of the world. A town built on a hill cannot be hidden. Neither do people light a lamp and put it under a bowl. Instead they put it on its stand, and it gives light to everyone in the house. In the same way, let your light shine before others, that they may see your good deeds and glorify your Father in heaven."

MATTHEW 5:14-16

A CITY ON A HILL CANNOT BE HIDDEN

Light is impossible to ignore.

In the dead of night, even the smallest candle is noticeable.

In total darkness, a single flame changes everything.

Jesus knew this when He said:

"You are the light of the world. A town built on a hill cannot be hidden."

This isn't just an encouragement, it's a declaration.

If you lead the Jesus Way, if your mind is renewed and transformed,

Your leadership will stand out.

Your presence will disrupt darkness.

Your influence will change the landscape around you.

But here's the key:

You don't have to force it.

Jesus never said:

> "Make yourself shine."

> "Promote your light."

> "Find a way to be seen."

He simply said:

"A town built on a hill cannot be hidden."

If we live the Jesus Way, Jesus positions us for impact.

If we remain faithful, Jesus places us where our light can be seen.

If we lead with righteousness, Jesus ensures our leadership illuminates the right path for others.

This means:

> You don't have to chase influence—Jesus will put you where you need to be.

You don't have to fight for a platform—when the time is right, your light will shine.

You don't have to fear being overlooked—Jesus never hides a light that He has ignited.

Leadership is always taking people somewhere.

And if you are light, your leadership will either guide people toward life,

Or let them remain in darkness.

Light doesn't just exist—

It guides.

It reveals.

It pulls people forward.

It whispers, "This is the way. Keep going."

That's what leadership does.

Not by shouting.

Not by forcing.

But by walking ahead—

Carrying clarity into the unknown.

Jesus calls us to lead as light.

Not light that flickers,

Not light that hides,

But light that gives direction.

LIGHT IS PLACED WITH PURPOSE

Jesus says, "Neither do people light a lamp and put it under a bowl. Instead they put it on its stand, and it gives light to everyone in the house."

He is teaching a leadership principle about placement here.

A light does not place itself.

A city does not build itself on a hill.

A lamp does not determine where it shines.

Someone places it there.

And this is the key to the Jesus Way of leadership:

Jesus is the one who positions you.

You don't have to:

> Manipulate your way into influence.

> Strive to make yourself seen.

> Force open doors before their time.

If you lead with the right mindset—

If you develop the right flavor of leadership—

Jesus will position you exactly where you need to be.

This means:

> You don't have to chase a title. Jesus will put you where your light is needed.

> You don't have to worry about being overlooked. Jesus doesn't waste light.

> You don't have to force recognition. When it's time to shine, the world will see.

This is what separates the Jesus Way from the world's way of leadership.

In the world, leaders fight for position.

In the kingdom, leaders are placed in position.

The only question is:

Will you be ready when Jesus places you?

WHY JESUS' POSITIONING MATTERS

The biggest mistake leaders make is trying to position themselves before they are ready.

> Some leaders chase platform before preparation.

> Some leaders chase power before character is formed.

Some leaders chase visibility before they've developed depth.

God never positioned people before they were ready.

Moses spent forty years in the wilderness before God positioned him to lead Israel.

David was anointed as king but spent years as a shepherd and fugitive before taking the throne.

Joseph had a vision of leadership but endured betrayal, slavery, and prison before he was positioned as Pharaoh's second-in-command.

God is not in a rush.

He will position you when your heart, mindset, and leadership are aligned with Him.

This means:

If you feel unseen, trust the process—Jesus is refining you.

If you feel like doors aren't opening, focus on growth—Jesus is preparing you.

If you feel impatient, remember—every great leader in Scripture had a season of waiting before their moment arrived.

Jesus doesn't waste leaders.

When you are ready, He will place you where you can have the greatest impact.

The real question isn't whether Jesus will position you.

It's whether you are becoming the kind of leader He can position.

LIGHT ON THE SHORE

The boat rocked quietly on the early morning water.

Peter squinted through the mist,

Hands rough from a long night of failure.

No fish.

No fire.

Just silence.

He had gone back to what he knew—

The nets, the water, the work—

Anything to drown out the memory

Of that courtyard fire

And the rooster's cry.

He told himself he was fine.

That it was over.

That maybe he had never really been called at all.

And then—

A voice.

"Friends, haven't you any fish?"

They hadn't.

"Throw your net on the right side of the boat and you will find some."

And suddenly—

The nets were full.

Just like the first time.

Just like the day He called them.

John leaned in and whispered what Peter's heart already knew.

"It is the Lord!"

Peter didn't wait.

He didn't hesitate.

He dove into the water

And ran toward the shore like a man who couldn't afford one more second of distance.

And there He was.

Jesus.

Standing by a fire—

Not of judgment,

But of charcoal and grace.

There was bread.

There was fish.

There was no sermon.

Just breakfast.

And when the meal was finished,

Jesus turned to Peter.

He didn't mention the denial.

He didn't repeat the rooster's crow.

He asked a question.

"Do you love me?"

Three times.

Not to shame—

But to restore.

Three wounds.

Three invitations.

"Feed my lambs."

"Take care of my sheep."

"Feed my sheep."

Jesus didn't just forgive Peter.

He gave him back his purpose.

He reminded him that failure doesn't end the call—

It refines it.

Peter thought the story was over.

But Jesus lit a new path—

One that began right there,

On that quiet shoreline,

Bathed in mercy,

Fueled by love,

And forever changed by light.

LOSING OUR LIGHT

Light doesn't disappear all at once.

It fades.

Flickers.

Pulls back, one compromise at a time.

Some leaders lose their light

Because they disconnect from the source.

They stop spending time with God.

They stop listening.

They stop abiding.

And when the connection is gone,

So is the clarity.

Some lose their light

Because they try too hard to blend in.

They water down their convictions

To avoid standing out.

But a hidden light can't help anyone.

It may feel safer in the shadows—

But no one is guided by silence.

Others lose their light

Because they lead from fear,

Not faith.

They protect their position

Instead of walking in purpose.

They forget they were placed to shine,

Not just survive.

Your light isn't just what you do—

It's who you reflect.

Stay close to the source.

Stay true to the calling.

Let the light burn bright.

THE LEADERSHIP REVOLUTION IS ABOUT VISIBILITY

Jesus didn't just call us to be light,

He positioned us to shine where we are needed most.

But here's the key:

Light is not about self-promotion.

The world tells leaders:

"Get seen."

"Make a name for yourself."

"Gain influence and power."

But Jesus says:

"I will place you."

"I will position you."

"I will determine where your light is needed most."

The difference?

One is man-made influence.

The other is God-placed impact.

And here's what matters most:

A light placed by God cannot be hidden.

A leader positioned by Jesus cannot be ignored.

A leadership revolution fueled by righteousness cannot be stopped.

This is why the Jesus Way isn't just another leadership model.

It's a movement that will reshape leadership as we know it.

But for this revolution to happen, leaders must be willing to:

Stand in the light.

Refuse to compromise.

Let Jesus position them instead of forcing themselves into influence.

This is the call of the Jesus Way.

CHAPTER SEVENTEEN

LIVING AS
SALT AND LIGHT

"You are the salt of the earth. But if the salt loses its saltiness, how can it be made salty again? It is no longer good for anything, except to be thrown out and trampled underfoot." "You are the light of the world. A town built on a hill cannot be hidden. Neither do people light a lamp and put it under a bowl. Instead they put it on its stand, and it gives light to everyone in the house. In the same way, let your light shine before others, that they may see your good deeds and glorify your Father in heaven."

MATHEW 5:13-16

IT'S NOT ENOUGH TO KNOW—WE MUST LIVE IT

The world is full of leaders who know the right things to do.

They've read the books.

They've heard the sermons.

They can talk about values, integrity, and leadership.

But the world doesn't need more leaders who know.

The world needs leaders who live differently.

This is what the Jesus Way demands.

Jesus didn't say:

> "You should try to be salt."

> "You might become light."

> "One day, you'll have influence."

He said:

> "You are the salt of the earth."

> "You are the light of the world."

This isn't a suggestion—it's an identity statement.

If you have a renewed mind, if you are leading with righteousness, mercy, and meekness,

Then your presence will be impossible to ignore.

And remember:

Being salt and light is not about a single moment. It's a way of living.

It's the result of thousands of daily choices—

How we respond, how we lead, how we serve, and how we love.

LIVING AS SALT AND LIGHT

Salt doesn't season itself.

Light doesn't shine for itself.

Salt exists to enhance.

Light exists to illuminate.

Jesus was clear—

Your leadership is not about you.

It's about those you serve.

Your influence is not for personal gain.

It's meant to lift others up.

This is the mindset shift of the Jesus Way.

Salt must touch what it seasons.

Light must be seen to guide.

That means showing up—

In conversations with encouragement.

In tension with righteousness.

In dark places with hope and truth.

And it's not just about the immediate.

Salt also preserves over time.

Light continues to guide long after the moment passes.

A kind word today may shape someone's confidence for years.

An act of integrity may ripple into generations.

A moment of mercy may transform a life.

This is what it means to live as salt and light—

Daily decisions that leave a lasting mark.

SALT AND LIGHT IN ONE ACT

The room was still.

The table set.

The hour heavy.

Jesus knew.

He knew the cross was close.

He knew the betrayal was coming.

He knew the hearts of those gathered—

Still full of ambition,

Still jostling for position,

Still unsure of what true greatness looked like.

So He got up.

Not to teach.

Not to command.

Not to perform a miracle.

But to serve.

He took off His outer garment.

Tied a towel around His waist.

And knelt.

One by one,

He cupped their dusty feet in His hands.

He poured the water.

He moved slowly.

Deliberately.

No one spoke.

Because this wasn't how kings acted.

This wasn't how leaders behaved.

This wasn't the way of the world.

But it was the way of heaven.

Peter squirmed.

"Lord, are you going to wash my feet?"

He couldn't reconcile it.

The Messiah. The Master. The Teacher—kneeling.

"You do not realize now what I am doing," Jesus said,

"But later you will understand."

And He was right.

Because in that moment, Jesus wasn't just washing feet.

He was seasoning their understanding.

He was preserving the purity of leadership.

He was illuminating what greatness really means.

Salt and light—

Poured out through water and towel.

Jesus reminds us that **leadership isn't about status.**

It's about service.

And when He was done, He stood.

Looked them in the eye.

And said:

"Now that I, your Lord and Teacher, have washed your feet,
you also should wash one another's feet."

He didn't just teach the Jesus Way.

He lived it—on His knees.

With His hands.

In the quiet, sacred act of love that changes everything.

THE LEADERSHIP REVOLUTION STARTS HERE

A renewed mind produces salt and light.

Salt and light produce leadership that cannot be ignored.

Leadership that cannot be ignored produces a revolution.

And here's the best part:

You don't have to wait to start.

You don't need a bigger platform.

You don't need a new position.

You don't need approval from the world.

You are already salt and light.

Jesus has already placed you somewhere to shine.

Now it's up to you:

> Will you choose to enhance, preserve, and create a thirst for righteousness?
>
> Will you step into your calling, knowing that your presence will shape the lives of those around you?
>
> Will you embrace the Jesus Way—not just as an idea but as a movement that will change leadership forever?

Because this is where the revolution begins.

CHAPTER EIGHTEEN

THE LEADERSHIP REVOLUTION HAS BEGUN

"Do not conform to the pattern of this world,
but be transformed by the renewing of your mind.
Then you will be able to test and approve what
God's will is—his good, pleasing and perfect will."
ROMANS 12:2

LIVE DIFFERENT AND LEAD DIFFERENT

Leadership is changing.

Not because of a new trend.

Not because of shifting workplace cultures.

Not because of a self-improvement movement.

But because **God is orchestrating a leadership revolution.**

For too long, leadership has been defined by power, control, and ego.

For too long, organizations have valued performance over people.

For too long, leaders have been trained to manage results instead of transform lives.

But that era is ending.

God is raising up a new kind of leader.

A leader with a renewed mind.

A leader who leads with peace, joy, purpose, and legacy.

A leader who cannot be ignored—because they are salt and light.

This is not just a better way to lead.

This is a movement.

And the time to step into it is now.

Look around.

The workplace is broken.

Employees are exhausted, undervalued, and disengaged.

Companies chase short-term wins instead of lasting impact.

Churches are struggling.

Many are full of leaders who preach one way but lead another.

Many are too afraid to challenge the status quo.

Communities are divided.

Leadership has become about platform over purpose.

About control over care.

The world does not need more leaders in title.

The world needs leaders in mindset.

Leaders who live the Jesus Way.

Leaders who have been transformed by the Beatitudes.

Leaders who have tasted the true rewards of leadership and refuse to settle for anything less.

Leaders who know that when they live with a renewed mind, Jesus positions them for impact.

The world needs leaders who are impossible to ignore.

Not because they chase attention.

But because their way of leading is radically different from the world.

This is the leadership revolution.

And it's already happening.

You don't need a title to be part of the leadership revolution.

You don't need a stage, a social media following, or a high-ranking position.

You don't need an invitation from the world to step into this calling.

You already have one—from Jesus.

Every interaction is an opportunity to be salt.

Every decision is an opportunity to be light.

Every moment is an opportunity to bring the Jesus Way to life.

This is how the revolution spreads.

It doesn't begin with policies or speeches.

It begins in the small moments when you choose to lead differently.

When you choose meekness over dominance.

When you choose mercy over retaliation.

When you choose purity of heart over personal gain.

When you choose peace over division.

When you choose to embrace persecution rather than compromise truth.

And when enough leaders step into this way of thinking…

Organizations will change.

Families will change.

The world will change.

THIS IS NOT JUST A BOOK—IT'S A MOVEMENT

The Jesus Way is not just a book.

It's not just a leadership method.

It's a revolution that will shake leadership at its core.

The only question is:

Will you be part of it?

You have everything you need.

The Beatitudes have shaped your mindset.

The rewards of leadership have shown you the fruit of leading this way.

Salt and light have revealed that this kind of leadership will transform the world.

Now it's time to step forward.

Because the world is waiting.

And the leadership revolution cannot happen without you.

Welcome to the revolution.

THE MINDSETS OF THE JESUS WAY

The Jesus Way is not about leadership techniques—it's about a renewed mind.

Jesus Way leaders do not lead through personal ambition, power, or ego.

Instead, they lead from transformed hearts and minds fully aligned with God.

These eight mindsets define the Jesus Way of leadership.

They shape how a leader thinks, moves, and impacts the world.

1. POOR IN SPIRIT

Key Phrase: We can't do it on our own.

Key Word: Dependence

Explanation: Leadership begins with surrender. Jesus Way leaders recognize that they cannot lead in their own strength. True leadership is built on dependence on God, not self-sufficiency.

2. MOURNING

Key Phrase: We don't carry it alone.

Key Word: Surrender

Explanation: Leaders in the Jesus Way don't suppress pain or shoulder burdens alone. They bring struggles to God, allowing Him to heal, strengthen, and transform their pain into wisdom and compassion.

3. MEEKNESS

Key Phrase: Never lose your strut.

Key Word: Trust

Explanation: Meekness is not weakness—it's a confident trust in God's timing and authority. Jesus Way leaders don't shrink back, force outcomes, or lead from ego. They walk with steady, humble confidence, knowing who they are in God.

4. HUNGER AND THIRST FOR RIGHTEOUSNESS

Key Phrase: We crave goodness in the world.

Key Word: Desire

Explanation: Jesus Way leaders aren't driven by power or success—they are driven by a desire to see goodness, justice, and righteousness prevail. They want what is right, not what is easy, and they fight for it in their leadership and influence.

5. MERCIFUL

Key Phrase: We lead with grace.

Key Word: Compassion

Explanation: Jesus Way leaders understand that mercy is power. Instead of leading with judgment or harshness, they extend grace, forgive easily, and lift others up.

6. PURE IN HEART

Key Phrase: A divided heart can't lead.

Key Word: Integrity

Explanation: Leadership in the Jesus Way demands singular focus—a heart fully aligned with God. A leader with a pure heart is free from ego, deceit, and personal ambition, leading with clarity and authenticity.

7. PEACEMAKERS

Key Phrase: We bring peace because we carry peace.

Key Word: Wholeness

Explanation: Leaders in the Jesus Way don't create conflict— they create unity. But true peace starts within. A peacemaker sets aside ego, judgment, and insecurity, leading with a spirit of reconciliation and strength.

8. PERSECUTED FOR RIGHTEOUSNESS

Key Phrase: We expect it, we accept it, and we move through it.

Key Word: Unshaken

Explanation: Leadership comes with resistance. Jesus Way leaders don't seek approval from the world—they expect opposition, accept it as part of the path, and move through it with unwavering focus on God. They don't fight back in fear—they stay firm in faith.

ABOUT THE AUTHOR

Casey Putney is a leadership focussed writer, speaker, trainer, and retired Air Force veteran who spent over twenty years leading teams across military, government, and corporate sectors. With a master's degree in leadership, global development experience, and credentials from Duke University and the John Maxwell Team, Casey has helped shape leaders at every level.

Today, Casey helps leaders move beyond influence—to impact—by aligning how they lead with who God created them to be.